WHY I DIDN'T SAVE THE WORLD

A Survivor's Story of Rape, Life, and Post-Traumatic Stress Disorder

by

Patricia Lawrence

No Simple Hiway Press

Why I Didn't Save the World:
A Survivor's Story of Rape, Life, and Post-Traumatic Stress Disorder

Published in the United States by No Simple Hiway Press

Book and cover design: Vladimir Verano, Third Place Press
www.thirdplacepress.com

ISBN: 978-0-9986695-0-2

Publisher Contact:
No Simple Hiway Press
Nosimplehiwaypress@gmail.com

For Grace, as promised

Author's Note

This is a true story. While it is told with dedication to the accuracy of facts as far as memory will permit, in some instances, minor details have been altered to facilitate storytelling. Names have been omitted to protect the guilty and the privacy of those involved through no fault of their own.

Preface

I like to tell stories. This one is mine. As do most storytellers, I like my stories to be heard and hope in the hearing welcomed, but most of all, I hope they will be helpful. I would so like this story to be helpful.

The telling of this tale began as an apology to my children, an attempt to explain my cruelty and my failures. Writing to the ones I loved, trying to explain what it was, how it was, even as the why of it eluded me, I wrote seeking forgiveness.

In the scheme of things, I know it doesn't matter whether or not I tell this story, that in truth this telling remains an effort to justify myself, my Self, but in the telling, I look for understanding in the tale.

CHAPTER 1

On Just A Smile

Memorial Day, 1971

The outhouse stinks. I kick open its filthy door with the toe of my cowboy boot and lunge outside, buttoning my bell-bottom jeans as the door slams shut behind me. A bead of sweat trickles down my forehead. Beyond the outhouse, surrounding the dilapidated filling station, desert grass shimmers in the mid-day sun.

I lift my long hair off my neck hoping to cool down. Gazing out at the desolate landscape, savoring the solitude, I consider abandoning my traveling companions here. For the last hundred miles, J's sung the same two verses of "Southern Man" in high falsetto and he deserves to die. K may as well go too.

Watching a butterfly perch lightly on a purple thistle, I release my hair and give up the idea of abandoning the boys. As appealing as the idea is at the moment, we are bound by rules of the road. The Age of Aquarius is underway; our code hails more from Crosby, Stills, and Nash than Kerouac. I turn away from the open desert and head back to the front of the filling station.

Approaching the gas pumps, my stomach lurches at the sight of K on his back under our ride, an old Ford van, a pool of water spreading out around him. J stands away, hands on hips, avoiding the enlarging puddle.

"It's the freeze plug." K's voice drifts out from under the van.

I have no idea what a freeze plug is, but this is the second time K has blamed a puddle on it, and with his assessment, my last hope of making it home for my twentieth birthday vanishes.

K slides himself out from under and stands up, wiping his hands on his jeans. "We can't leave it here. We've gotta get it out of the way." He motions to the edge of the parking lot.

This isn't the first time we've had to push the old van. We know the drill. J and I take our places at either door. K pushes from behind. I steer and push. K groans from the effort. J is useless. Eventually the van comes to rest at the lot's edge.

We stand silent in the gravel parking lot among the few dusty pick-up trucks waiting for their drivers, each lost in our own version of the problems facing us. We haven't much left to say to one another. Our attempt to get back to Hawaii, where we first met several months ago, isn't going well.

Since leaving Hawaii, K and I have been in Colorado, intending to move on to Vermont to set up a hide-out for draft dodgers. J's been in New York. The frigid winter convinces all of us that we're making a terrible mistake, and we decide to return to Hawaii, J joining us in Denver for the drive west.

I'd hoped to be in California tomorrow to spend my birthday with family before catching a plane to Hawaii, but we're now stranded on a rural highway outside Salt Lake City and that hope just slipped away.

I lean back against the van staring at nothing. The filling station has a garage, but it's closed for the Memorial Day holiday, though we have no money for repairs in any case. I have only enough for gas to California and airfare to Honolulu, and the boys never seem to have any extra of their own.

A small café, its cardboard "Open" sign leaning in the front porch window, shares the parking lot. Ramshackle tin sheds line the other side of the highway. Otherwise, nothing but tumbleweeds occupies this stretch of road. There will be nowhere to hide if we're stuck here overnight.

This isn't Denver or San Francisco; the boys' long hair stirs up the locals. They freeze as we pass by, watching each move we make until we're safely away. Last night, men in pickups chased us out of a diner parking lot and stayed on our tail for miles down the highway. Finally, frightened and unable to shake them off, we took refuge in a motel where the desk clerk reluctantly agreed to rent us a room as the pursuing trucks spun donuts in his parking lot.

Adrenaline, regret, and creeping desperation kept me awake. I stayed up most of the night sitting on the bathroom floor, leaning against the bathtub, reading the Gideon's Bible I found in a bedside drawer. J & K shared the bed.

Leaving the motel this morning, muddled from my sleepless night—but the only licensed driver—I drove miles in the wrong direction, missing the Interstate exit and bringing us instead to this spot on a small highway in Tooele County where we are now stuck, surrounded by more pickups.

Settling down on the cement curb fronting the café, I consider our options, but I have no ideas left. Folding my arms on my knees, I rest my head on top of those.

Life on the road is not as exotic as the songs imply, becoming myself having proven more difficult to accomplish than the song lyrics might suggest. I dropped out of college before leaving on this adventure and regret is consuming me. As a student at UH, all I needed to do was attend class and wear sunscreen. Now, instead of luxuriating in warm sand and tropical water, I'm stranded amid seared desert scrub.

Lacing fingers through my hair, I bury my face in my knees. A tear slides through the dust on my face and drips onto the grey and black gravel at my feet.

I'd been unable to explain to family why I dropped out of college. Tensions were high when I drove away, headed for Vermont. I had hoped they would welcome me home for my birthday, that it might be the beginning of reparations. I don't believe I can call them now for help. I left under a cloud and this mess is mine.

I hadn't planned to go away to college. My mother married as I graduated from high school and moved with Little Sis to a new home in Atherton. I had hoped to be part of the new family. I planned to go to Foothill College and to share a new life with my sister and new step-siblings, but tensions abound in the blended household, and having grown up as a middle child with a single, working parent, I'm a bit too independent for the newly-structured group. Soon invited to attend college elsewhere, I choose UH Manoa. I love Hawaii; it smells of plumeria, and they don't require the SAT.

All the new family comes to Waikiki to help settle me in. We find student housing: an apartment share with three other girls close to campus. My new stepfather buys me a red, convertible VW Bug. Then the family returns home to California, leaving me to grow up.

So far, growing up has been as a child of the Sixties. With no dad, and a mom who worked long hours, I have enjoyed freedom, if not maturity.

I wish upon stars, believe All You Need is Love, and don't trust anyone over thirty. And although I'm a good student, my highest priority is reveling in the music blooming around me. I've spent my weekends swirling amidst the psychedelic lightshows at Avalon Ballroom and Fillmore West, and dancing in Golden Gate Park with flowers in my hair. My heroes are the Grateful Dead, Santana, and Janis Joplin. I've watched the Beatles sing "I Wanna Hold Your Hand" at the Cow Palace, the Stones rage through "Get Off My Cloud" at the San Jose Civic Auditorium, and Jimi Hendrix alter reality at Winterland.

I believe in Peace, Love, and Brotherhood. I believe This Is It. I am a student of my cosmic responsibility. We are special. We are brilliantly alive. I pity the conservative, dismissing convention as ignorance, and I cling to this credo, despite being witness to the chaos at Altamont.

I am not alone. I disregard social convention from personal need, my home life being a little off-kilter, and my peers, for reasons of their own, are doing the same. As a group, we rebel.

We wear prohibited jeans to school day after day until we're allowed to wear them. We refuse to recite the Pledge of Allegiance until we don't have to recite it. We refuse to tuck in our shirts or to keep our hair trimmed until we don't have to do that either. We are insufferable, but passionate.

We protest the Vietnam War, raging through Lytton Plaza taunting police, fists raised, shouting "Hell No, We Won't Go." My first boyfriend goes to prison straight from high school rather than to war. I believe we are in the right, and that I know just about everything there is to know.

So, when left to my own devices in Waikiki, I do what the occasion calls for: I go to the beach. Within days of the family's departure, I abandon the apartment with the girls (whom I never meet) and rent an apartment with a boy I attract while lying in the warm Waikiki sand. He catches my eye one afternoon and leaves the girl whose towel he shares to share mine instead. G has been studying yoga in a Canadian ashram and looks like an Episcopal Jesus.

We rent a studio apartment done in floral prints and rattan on the fifth floor of a circular tower near the Ala Moana Shopping Center, soon known to us as the Spaceship. We hang Indian bedspreads on the walls and a beaded curtain in the hall.

1970 Hawaii is a mecca for flower children and the willfully disenfranchised. Landward is not yet high-rise hell. The Marketplace is not walled-in, but sprawls haphazardly under the Indian banyan and into the sunshine. The streets aren't crowded, but busy and fluid. Wandering innocents, smelling of patchouli and wearing little except nose-rings and long hair, stand in small groups or alone, intoning requests for spare change. Enchanted, one by one, I invite them to live with me, until eleven of us share the studio apartment.

I want to be just like them. I want to stroll down Kalakaua Avenue in a white sarong with Jesus sandals and gold hoop earrings, stopping to chat casually with suntanned beach boys about the next free concert at the Shell or the Hari Krishna breakfasts, and though I never master their casual manner, I offer the flower children what I have: a place to stay. I love them all. I want them to be my family.

We range in age from fifteen to twenty-five. The youngest is a runaway, the eldest a poet. K and J stay most nights—K a draft dodger whose chestnut hair sweeps his shoulders, J his graceful albino sidekick.

Two other apartments in the building serve as havens like mine, with tenants sharing meals and sleeping partners. The Doors and Moody Blues serenade us day and night. Occasionally, sailors on R&R from Vietnam drift in and stay a few days. Once in a while, one returns for a second stay. Those who do seem always less alive, the war itself killing them before they die.

The apartment has an entry hall off the circular elevator lobby, bath and closet off that, with living, sleeping, and kitchen in the one room at the end of the hall. The facing wall, a plate glass sliding-door, opens onto a modest balcony. The balcony looks out toward the ocean, too far for details, but the immense deep blue stretches to our horizon.

Wooden stools front the kitchen workspace. A convertible sofa serves for daytime seating, and at night its cushions are spread about the floor. Sleeping bags and blankets serve those of us who miss a prime lie-down opportunity. I have no status as the landlord and take my chances each evening, as does everyone else.

Nights are warm and restless. I'm the only student, seemingly the only person with a schedule to keep, although J & K claim to be making tortillas for a living. Real sleep is a luxury found at dawn on the beach for those of us who need it.

Everyone in the apartment claims to be a vegetarian, as are all enlightened beings of the time. I fast and follow fashion, but sneak out occasionally to the Food Court in the belly of the Ala Moana Shopping Center, where in secret I wolf down tomato-beef chow mein.

G and I are not a good match. We tolerate one another for a few weeks, and then he drifts off. Before leaving, he brings home a friend—bandy legs and dreadlocked blond hair. He stays.

One afternoon, in what seems to me to be a random tirade, the newcomer takes offense at a perceived sexual rebuff. I am not engaged with anyone at this point. I'm oblivious to this as a problem. He, however, is under the impression that once he leaves the apartment, I have sex with everyone else.

He uses a kitchen stool to express his pique, intending to take out the plate-glass sliding door. As he swings the stool, I interpose myself, believing that should he shatter the door, my stepfather will not appreciate the repair bill or understand the address for it. I have no choice but to take the hit.

Years later, I mistakenly unhook a fellow scuba diver's weight-belt and sink to the floor of Monterey Bay clutching it, thinking that I cannot let go even if I drown because I can't afford to replace it. This is the same sort of reasoning: painful and short-sighted.

The stool breaks across my back, knocking me out. When I revive, everyone seems to think I should leave for a little while. Too disabled to think this through, I do leave, but later as I sit outside I wonder why I left, this being my apartment, and even though I am not, I could be sleeping with everyone there if I wanted to be. In truth, I'm a little disappointed that it isn't even remotely true.

And my new family is not what I hoped.

Soon after, nearing the end of my first semester at UH, I sit cross-legged on the couch trying to make sense of Malaysian shadow puppets. Class registration at UH began alphabetically by academic seniority. As a freshman with a Y surname, by the time it was my turn, there were few class choices left. At registration, frustrated to tears by the lack of options, I finally pieced together a schedule that includes a graduate seminar on Southeast Asian history. No one seems concerned that I'm a freshman with no academic background in the subject.

A few weeks into the seminar, I'm delighted when a married couple invites me to study with them. They come over to the apartment, and we review a bit of lecture. They then invite me to participate in a ménage-a-trois. I decline, and the study group dissolves, but the class turns out to be fascinating, if a bit awkward, and since we are at war in the region, brutally relevant.

I have the apartment to myself this afternoon as I ponder the cultural significance of puppetry in Southeast Asian history. It's unusual to be alone here for long, so I'm not surprised when a neighbor pushes through the clattering bead curtain and strolls down the hall. The front door is never locked; there are too many of us.

I recognize the young man who saunters in. He's a flight attendant and rumored-to-be coke dealer, a bit too tan, too groomed. We've never spoken. He holds an open beer.

"D here?"

"No, at the beach, I think."

He finishes the beer and crumples the can. "Trash?"

"Under the sink." I point in its direction, still sitting on the couch. After tossing the empty can, he comes around to stand in front of me. He stands too close.

I pick my textbook back up, resting it on my lap, "I don't know where he is."

"Who?"

"D."

"Oh, yeah." He bounces slightly on the balls of his feet then steps closer, his legs now pressing against my knees.

I try to shift my legs away from his, but he blocks the effort, sliding forward until his intentions are in my face. I realize the misperception must extend beyond the apartment.

"No, no. Sorry." I am, truly. I'm sorry for the misunderstanding. The apology is sincere. I squirm, trying for more distance.

I find none, and my reluctance enrages him. He backhands my face so hard I'm knocked off the couch to the floor. My sundress is off, and he's on top of me while I'm still hanging in the force of the slap. For a moment, he fumbles uselessly with himself, then hits me again. His spirit is willing, but it's a no-go from the body.

Raging at his own impotence, he grabs me by the hair and drags me across the room out onto the balcony. Stumbling, crab-walking backwards, I slap and tear at his hands as he drags me through the door and hurls me against the balcony railing, trying to toss me over it.

Entwining arms and legs through the metal railing, I grip everything I can hold onto as he fights with me. I hope someone will look up, and then desperately hope no one does. I know I need to cry for help, but what do I do if The Man shows up? We can't stand the scrutiny; some of us are outlaws and Stepfather will be so pissed.

I hang on as he claws at my arms and fingers trying to pry them loose. Finally, giving up on them, he grabs my hair instead, jerking my head back and snarling at me through clenched teeth. I stare at him, frozen, my startled whimper struggling to become a scream, when with even less warning than at its onset, the attack is over. His grip loosens, his face relaxes, and he lets me go.

It seems a switch has flipped. Wherever he's been, he's back. Staring at me as if he's never seen me before and is surprised to see me hanging there, he backs away, finally turning to pick up his shorts and stepping into them on his way through the apartment. I hold onto the railing until the cackle of the beaded curtain lets me know he's gone.

I don't report the assault. My family can't know—my living situation being difficult to explain—and Police are Pigs. My roommates are casual in their concern and lack thereof. It seems understood that I must have been at fault. At the very least, I'm a tease.

A few days later, I'm evicted from the apartment for making too much noise.

Soon after telling my communal family of the eviction, they vanish. Except for J & K, I lose all contact. And with a few weeks left until the end of the school semester, but only a few days before eviction is final, I need a new home too, but can't face explaining why to my mother or new stepfather. The first is too troubled and the second too respectable.

K and I spend his twenty-first birthday in Kapiolani Park under the shower tree canopy. Feds are hanging out in the apartment lobby, and though we aren't certain what lured them there, K, wanted for draft evasion, is reluctant to return. We make a tent of palm fronds and sit watching the night. Before long, I realize I've found an option for my new home. The next morning, I buy a pup tent and pitch it at Hanauma Bay.

The Bay is not yet a nature preserve. Camping is free and allowed six weeks at a time. A small contingent of the motley and penniless live here full time, packing up for a day or two when the park rangers come by on their routine rousting patrol.

I set up on the farthest tip of Sandman's Patch and study for finals sitting on a rock outside the tent, leaning on the sun-warmed boulders at the edge of the surf. My immediate neighbors are two young panhandlers who teach me camp etiquette and invite me to play volleyball. K stays with me sometimes. J has returned to New York.

One pristine night, a king tide brings the ocean rising silently up into our tents. We scramble from our sleeping bags and stand in the crystal light of the full moon, shadow figures at the rim of the horseshoe bay, and watch the water recede as silently as it advanced, leaving behind small boulders to mark where it has been without more than a ripple of surf at its edge.

My final grades are good. I get an A in the graduate course.

The bruises on my face and arms heal, but a deeper bruise, unrelated to skin or muscle or blood, embeds itself on the fabric of my Self. I no longer want to watch the sunsets. I don't want to swim or sunbathe or study, and I ignore registration for the second semester.

I find no way to explain to family why I'm dropping out of school. I am embarrassed by memory of the attack because it had been, I'm fairly certain, my own fault—living with boys, wearing skimpy clothes, letting a stranger into the apartment. I let the details sink away and leave Hawaii in December 1970, going home to California uncertain of my reception and with no clear idea of what to do next.

Before I leave Hawaii, K invites me to come with him to Vermont to set up a sanctuary for draft dodgers. I tell him I'll consider it.

I haven't explained dropping out to myself either, except as a vague dissatisfaction, homesickness the best explanation I have, and not entirely satisfied, my mother and stepfather allow me a room in the new home only until I "make a plan."

The first night in this room, my new stepbrothers leave a live potato bug on my pillow. The huge insect crawls into my hair, and I hurl it out the second-story window, hoping it lands gently on the lawn below despite its terrifying aspect. We still are not a happily blended family.

Stepfather soon asks me to leave. The only plan I've come up with is to live at home and go to community college. He tells me I can't stay. I accept K's invitation to go with him to Vermont.

I cash in my one savings bond to buy a 1964 Ford Econoline van, and K and I set off from Atherton heading to Vermont with sixteen dollars cash, a double bed mattress on the floorboards, and a handmade Yin Yang flag hanging in the back window. We are on a mission: Hell No, We Won't Go. Make Love, Not War. We are saving the world.

We live off what we panhandle, buying gasoline and food—usually milk, Beefaroni, and canned peas. K's teeth suffer from long neglect and eating is difficult for him. None of these foods need much chewing, and institutional-sized canned peas sell for pennies.

It's winter so we first head south, then drive through Arizona, stopping to shower in college dorms and to beg for spare change on street corners, before heading into the Rockies. As we climb into the mountains, the van is heroic, but ill-suited to the elevation, laboring at times to a crawl. It finally breaks down in Denver where, for the first time, K blames the freeze plug.

Water pools beneath us when we stop for gas at a station on Colfax Avenue. K says we can't go farther until the van is fixed, but with no money for repairs, we push it around the corner onto a residential street of fenced yards and old trees and settle in.

We live in the van, staying as best we can in the back, out of sight. The temperature hovers near freezing; snow piles up on the streets and sidewalks. Our frozen breath laces the windows, and the door locks freeze solid. We learn to cup our hands and breathe on the locks until they thaw to let ourselves in and out as the needs arise.

Parking in the neighborhood where we have broken down is time-restricted and rigorously enforced. Police both ticket and boot vehicles. The boot, a metal clamp bolted to a tire, doesn't come off until the fine is paid. Fines are out of the question. As far as I know, K has nothing. I have nothing. We get out and push the van a few feet forward or back every few hours; the frozen streets crispy under our feet as we seek purchase and strength.

The sidewalk has a grassy strip between curb and walkway which serves as the occasional urinal, our only option being a walk down the block to the White Spot coffee shop. Night walks in freezing weather discourage the trip. I wet the bed only once, a special problem when the bed is a mattress in the back of a van on a frozen city street, and I regret it for quite some time. From then on, a quick squat on the curb isn't quite as noxious.

The White Spot and its facilities, Formica and chrome swivel stools at the counter, steak and eggs with white toast on the plates, serve us for a few weeks before we move to the transient hotel nearby. K and I show up at the restaurant once or twice a day, sometimes heading straight in and out, sometimes stopping for soup or coffee to keep our visits honest. An older waitress with a wavy ponytail takes a fancy to us, romanticizing the adventure, and extends kindness. She is soft-spoken and eager to support our quest, inviting us home for a meal and use of her shower.

We can't survive solely on panhandling here; too many others are doing the same. If we are to eat, finding paid employment quickly becomes critical.

My options for a work wardrobe are limited. I own only a grey wool v-neck sweater, a blue T-shirt, my Levi bell-bottoms with hand-sewn paisley flare inserts, and tan slip dress. A pair of Keds, Frye cowboy boots, or flip flops will complete the outfit. Jobs suitable to these limited options are difficult to come by, but rather than starve, I set out roaming the streets to find one.

Neither do I have a telephone number or address.

Asking for work on street corners is sketchier than asking directly for money. Misunderstandings occur. But once I adjust my approach, I find work as a telemarketer in the back of a fifth-wheeler, pitching vacation scams to seniors. I last a few hours before the despicable work sends me back onto the street.

Down the road, the neighborhood movie theater is hiring. My apparel is appropriate and the young, male manager doesn't require an address. I sell popcorn and candy at the concession counter and eat my fill of Junior Mints.

The theater manager and ticket seller are engaged, both just out of high school and on their way. The ticket seller invites K and me to her apartment for dinner. She is quiet and sweet and seems to find us a bit exotic.

Unfortunately, even with Junior Mints thrown in, the weekly paycheck for four hours of work at $1.35 an hour does not stretch far. K stays under cover, avoiding the draft and those busy enforcing it, but I look again and find better paying employment: food waitress at Azar's Big Boy restaurant.

This is a good career choice; they provide a uniform. They also train and supervise, a rare experience of excellence I appreciate fully only somewhat later in life.

With salary and tips, I earn enough for us to move out of the van and into the transient hotel on the corner: rooms by the hour, bathroom down the hall.

Our room has a black and white television set with rabbit ears, a water pitcher and bowl, and a faux mantel that holds a tape player with our single remaining tape: Joe Cocker. At the far end of the room, a mullion-windowed door leads onto a small balcony bounded by black-iron railings, open to Colfax Avenue one story below.

The hotel is populated by stoned working girls, and those who make this possible, generally a lost and soft-spoken lot. One afternoon, one of these residents, a young man, bursts through our door, throws a baggie of white powder on the bed, leaps onto the balcony and over the railing, dropping to the street below and running out of sight. K and I are still staring at the baggie when police dash in, guns drawn. Without a word, we point to the window and out they leap too. As advised, we are living outside the law being honest, if not entirely forthcoming. From the mantel, Cocker's cover of "She Came in through the Bathroom

Window" plays in the background. A few days later, the young man returns and retrieves the baggie.

I work nights at the restaurant, walking to and from work down Colfax Avenue. Many of the girls on the street are my neighbors at the hotel. They are dead-eyed, but kind to me, and hand me off corner to corner, before I head downhill behind the Capitol Building to the restaurant. The girls are spooked sometimes—I never know by what—then they walk with me the whole way, hurrying us from streetlight to streetlight until I am inside the restaurant or back at the hotel.

I'm assaulted on the walk only once. As I cross a street, a furtive young man runs into the crosswalk, grabs me and pinches my breasts several times. A light snow is falling, and I struggle to fend him off without dropping my clean waitress uniform in the wet snow. I can't show up for work with nothing to wear.

The girls come to my rescue, shouting and chasing him off. When I get to work and change into my uniform, my breasts are covered with purple bruises. The uniform is unharmed.

I enjoy waitressing. Patrons tip me well and benefits include a meal. With my first paycheck I must buy shoes (Keds fail completely as waitress shoes), but once my feet stop aching, I excel.

Our manager is buxom, smart, and good at her job. With her professional success, she hopes to redeem herself from the shame of an unwed pregnancy. Another co-worker is losing confidence in her dreams. The unconventional nature of my life reassures her. She tells me she finds my adventure to be proof that we make our own rules, that everything is possible.

I work the wee hours and find myself wondering what those customers who show up in these hours could possibly be doing during the day. Many I can't imagine finding anywhere else in the wider world.

Once a month, just before midnight, a seeming Jack Spratt and his wife come in. He is a tiny stick, his head barely reaching to the level of the table, and she is of grand proportion. She orders several full meals and cleans each plate. He nibbles at a few bites. They enter and leave hand-in-hand, disappearing down the road, into the darkness, after their lopsided banquet. Love is inexplicable, at best.

Another regular patron suffers from multiple sclerosis. A composer, he sits alone at a small table, nursing black coffee, struggling to finish work on his last symphony. Tremors rack his arms and hands as he fights to pen each tiny symbol, his concentration excruciating. He insists that the illness will not defeat him before the work is complete.

One regular, grizzled and grey, comes in each night and seats himself at the counter, laying his few coins down on the counter top and laboriously counting them out. He then spends a long time looking at the menu, seemingly deciding what to have. Usually, he can afford only coffee, but some days soup too. Most of us serve him soup anyway.

This man has grand mal epilepsy. When served, his pills are laid carefully before him ready to swallow with the water we bring. One night a seizure throws him off his counter stool to the floor. Seemingly before he lands, the fry cook vaults over the burners from the kitchen into the restaurant, lifting the seizing man and carrying him to the break room, laying him on the couch to wait for medical help. I love these people and am privileged to work with them.

But as winter turns to a chill spring, the damp, the grime, and the walk down the hall to the bathroom wear us down. K and I abandon our mission to set up a sanctuary in Vermont, and decide instead to return to Hawaii. Despite our best intentions, other draft evaders will have to survive without our help.

I've saved my tips from waiting tables, and when the time comes, at the first bank that will accept them (not the first bank I stagger into lugging the pile wrapped in my skirt), I trade in the mounds of rolled coins for more portable paper bills, and we push the van back around the corner to the gas station for repairs—the freeze plug as I understand it.

Once the van is repaired, J reappears, joining us in Denver for the return trip west to San Francisco. We have made it to the Great Salt Lake desert when those repairs fail us, and we find ourselves stuck in Tooele County, Utah, this Memorial Day, the final day of my nineteenth year.

CHAPTER 2

The Rabbit Hole

Before K, J, and I departed Denver on this stalled journey, I called my mother from the payphone in the hotel hallway and told her that I expected to be home for my birthday. She sounded pleased. Now, sitting on the curb in the hot sun, I toy with the idea of telephoning again and asking her for help, maybe forgiveness could begin right away.

I relax a little, brushing away the tears dripping down my face. No one will comfort me here; tears are worse than useless. As I wipe my face, pondering phoning my mother, K calls to me from across the lot.

He and J stand next to a VW bus, talking to two men. The two survey me as I get up and walk over to join them.

"These guys'll take us into the next town." K waits for my response. "We might find a freeze plug."

Once I join the group, neither of the two men looks directly at me. They glance and look away as I grapple with an answer. One man is obese, red hair and lips his only thin features, the latter taut in a smile or grimace, I can't tell which. The other man standing with the group towers over all of us, thuggish and grim. His jeans hang too low, offering glimpses of frayed underwear and hairy belly.

I step away, struggling for a way to politely decline the offer, "No, thanks... We haven't... We..." Excuses fail me. My voice trails off.

K pitches in, sounding relieved that I'm declining, "Yeah, thanks. We've got some other stuff..."

Neither man seems fazed by the brush off. "Okay, sure. We'll be inside if you change your minds." The redhead nods and the two men head up the stairs into the café without a second glance.

J watches the men climb the stairs. "Maybe we should have..." He hesitates, staring after them as the café's screen door slams shut.

"No." K doesn't elaborate, but it's clear he doesn't want to go anywhere with these two men either.

The afternoon is wearing on, and after the events of the previous evening, I'm sure we won't be safe here, out in the open, overnight. On vibes alone, I'm certain we didn't want their help, but I, too, wonder if declining was the right choice. We need help. They offered. They were creepy, but they offered. Maybe we made a mistake.

K resumes rummaging around underneath the crippled van. I assume he hasn't yet given up on the idea that he may singlehandedly and without tools effect repairs sufficient to put us back on the road. I figure I have a few minutes left before having to commit to calling my mother and confessing that I am not handling my life very well, that I am perhaps in physical danger, or that my two long-haired companions most certainly are. This last makes the explanation difficult, and I dread the looming conversation, but I can't leave them here. We who are on the road must have a code, and all that.

I drift back to the curb in front of the café and sit down again, hugging my knees. I'm tired and, aside from calling home, cannot figure a way out of here. We need a mechanic and car parts we don't have and can't afford. In their absence, we're going to need safe shelter. I just may have to call, beg, and face the disapproval. There seems no way around it.

The café's screen door bangs open on the porch behind me. For a moment, the rustle of dishware and conversation drifts in the air, cut off abruptly as the door slams shut. Exiting diners thump down the stairs behind me. One wears polished, black cowboy boots. I see them from the corner of my eye as they pass beside me. I don't raise my head, continuing to stare at the gravel at my feet as the boots crunch past.

A few minutes later, once again K calls to me. I rise to the summons.

Two new strangers stand talking to the boys. These men appear a bit less menacing than the first two: one tall and lanky, the other compact and spare. The latter wears the black boots. As I approach, both smile at me.

"These guys can take us into Salt Lake to look for an auto shop that might be open." K sounds pleased.

"Yeah, I have a friend…" offers the lanky one.

After the hostility that has greeted us everywhere since leaving Denver, I'm taken aback. I've come to expect men in these parts to be belligerent jerks but perhaps I misjudged them. Within minutes of being stranded here, four strangers have offered to help. To my surprise, Peace, Love, and Brotherhood may very well be blossoming even here in the desert.

"That would help us a lot." I smile. Both quickly look away without acknowledging my thanks, their attention shifting to K & J. I am dismissed. I assume this is now car repair talk, and I'm considered useless. Drifting away again, coming to rest a few feet away, I lean against the old van as the males continue their discussion.

As the four talk, the first two men to have offered us help, those whose offer we declined, come out of the café and join the conversation. The redhead extends a hand to the black boots and they perform introductions all around. I ignore them, pleased now that I will soon be on my way. I imagine a birthday party with family and swimming again in Waikiki's gentle surf.

While I'm daydreaming, the men decide that we ought to cover two directions in our search for a freeze plug. I am not alone in being surprised by the generosity of these strangers. K and J have dropped their hesitation about the first two men also. Now, they've decided that some of us will go into Salt Lake City to look for an open auto shop, and the rest will go into Grantsville, the next town down the highway.

Someone suggests that J, K, and I will go with the redhead and thug in the VW bus, and then "we'll all meet back here."

I don't notice who makes the suggestion, but I'm uneasy. I want to say I'll wait here with my van, but all the details, apparently, have been worked out while I diddled around ignoring them. I'm expected to go along.

Boots and his lanky companion head for the maroon pick-up truck, the others towards the bus. I decide I'm more afraid to stay here alone than to stick with K & J, and after stuffing our remaining money into my jeans' pocket rather than leave it unattended in the van, I join them by the VW.

Thug slides open the side door. "You guys sit back here." His voice is a deep rumble.

"Thanks." K steps inside. J & I follow.

The rear compartment is empty except for a wooden slat bench across the back. Floral curtains, large swirls of orange sunflowers and blue forget-me-nots, cover the windows.

I sit between the two boys on the hard bench. The door rolls shut, locking into place with a solid thud. I strain a little to see my van through the front windshield, hoping it will be safe left unattended.

Red grunts as he hoists his bulk into the driver's seat. Thug slides smoothly into the passenger side. Each slams his door shut. The Volkswagen engine turns over with its high-pitched whine, and we pull out of the parking lot onto the narrow highway, spewing gravel behind us.

We ride in silence. My eyes roam, trying to avoid meeting the driver's eye in the rear view mirror as he flicks repeatedly between looking ahead and checking behind. No one speaks. The silence becomes a presence, like the heat and the engine's hum. One of the men is wearing Old Spice. I decide it must be Red. Thug doesn't look like the type to worry about aftershave.

Minutes pass. I relax a little. The bench is too hard and I shift my weight to sit a little sideways.

"Sorry." I nearly knock J off his end. He purses his lips. I suspect he wishes he'd never left New York.

As we resettle ourselves, while I mutter apologies to smooth J's feathers, Red stops watching us in the mirror and turns his head to look at Thug. They hold the stare a long time and as they do, my small fluttering voice, the one that whispered "No" when I first met these two, now begins to scream. Panic floods my stomach, my arms, my legs. I have to get out of here. I have to get out of here *right now,* but I am not getting out. I am too late.

Red turns back to watch the road. Thug opens the glove compartment and pulls something out. In one motion, he turns all the way around in his seat to aim a pistol at the three of us, its hammer clicking as he cocks it back.

We are suspended. There is no air to breath, no sound to hear. The barrel of the gun seems to extend the length of the van, its pitch black bore filling all remaining space.

"On the floor, on your stomachs," he growls and steps over the seat into the back, keeping the gun pointed at us.

This is the moment we rear up and knock the gun from his hand, the three of us thrashing him to the floor, one of us leaping into the front seat, wresting control from the driver. But the three of us are paralyzed. The moment passes unseized. Without protest, we each lift ourselves slowly from the bench and lie down silently, obediently, on the floor.

"Hands behind your backs." Thug pulls duct tape from his pocket and begins binding K's feet and hands together behind his back. After taping K, he grabs my arms and twists each, pulling wrists to ankles. I don't react; I'm frozen, trying very hard to disappear. Finishing with me, he moves on to J.

I lie on my stomach, my back arched from the stretch of ankles bound to wrists, one cheek pressed against the gritty bus floor. K lies with his face turned toward me. My heart slamming in my chest, my mind reels in chaos.

"What do they want?" I mouth the words to him. He stares wide-eyed at me, giving me no other response. I plead silently for an explanation; having no idea what's coming makes it hard to keep breathing.

Thug finishes with J and sits down on the slat bench, one shoe pressing against my thigh. I try shifting out of the way, but have no leverage, no way to move except to rock up and down, and I don't want to call that much attention to myself.

The VW bus slows. My ear smacks the floor hard as we drop off the pavement and turn onto a dirt road, the hum of the wheels changing pitch. I start shivering. Resting my forehead on the floor, I try to remember a prayer, searching the floorboards for a savior.

The bus stops. Thug jerks the door handle, yanking the side door open. My eyes cringe shut at the sudden flood of light, opening again, reluctantly.

Just outside the van door, Boots and Lanks stand in the bright sun surveying us approvingly, the maroon pickup parked behind them.

"I'll get her." Thug steps over K and stands beside me. The gun hangs inches from my cheek, his hairy fingers wrapped around it. Gasping for breath, my heartbeat roaring in my ears, I try harder to disappear or to wake up.

Thug passes the gun out the door to Boots, who comes closer to take it. Deliberate and tense, squinting in the sunlight, the corners of his mouth pressed tight, he tests the gun's weight in his hand, pointing it at us, waving it back and forth slowly, as if choosing a target. Lanks stands loose beside him, an eager mongrel pup.

Thug unwraps my tape, freeing my arms and legs. I groan with relief in straightening them, but the relief is brief as he grabs my wrists and re-tapes them behind my back.

Within myself I am screaming, running, fighting to the death, but outside, I don't move a muscle. I know that I have to fight for my life *right now*. I know if I don't wake up or disappear *this moment* that I am lost, and still I can't do anything: I can't move, I can't breathe, yell, kick, nothing.

Thug lifts me by my arms and carries me out of the bus, standing me on wobbly legs beside it.

"Put a blindfold on her." Boots gives the order.

I stand quiet, shivering despite the heat, clutching a sliver of faith that this is a mistake. Yes, this is the best I've got. I grasp at hope that they will come to their senses, remember the rules we live by now: Make Love, Not War; Give Peace a Chance. They will mellow. The gun will be put away. We will laugh. They will apologize for being so uncool.

A bird trills overhead. Thug puts a piece of tape across my eyes, around my head, pulling my hair with it. With the blindness, I crumple; my middle collapses, my legs fold.

"No, you don't, honey." Lanks scoops me up and carries me to the pickup truck, struggling to open the door without dropping me, then dumping me on the seat inside.

I pull myself upright, scooting away as he settles on the seat beside me. The driver's door opens and a driver climbs in on my left. I assume it's Boots. Doors slam shut, the engine revs, and we pull out onto the dirt road leaving K, J, Red, and Thug behind.

"You put your head right down here, honey, out of sight." Lanks' voice is childish, almost playful. He grips the back of my neck and pushes my head down on his lap, my face shoved firmly against his crotch. I try not to inhale the sour stench. He begins stroking my hair, and hardens beneath my face. The hand stroking presses harder on the back of my head, pushing me more solidly against him.

Folded firmly into his lap, I hear traffic outside. We come to a brief stop and Lanks warns me to stay down, both hands holding me in place. Pressed into the sour darkness, Levi seams and zipper grinding against my face, I become Nancy Drew. Remembering every detective movie I've ever seen, I listen for clues. As the car moves again, I try tracking turns and counting passing cars. I listen for bells or other sounds I might use to identify our route. The hand on my head keeps stroking.

We travel forever—an hour, perhaps fifteen minutes—forever. I lose track of my clues. Traffic noise, evident for a while, fades. My world is diminished to musty darkness, body heat, my slamming heart, and the hand petting the back of my head.

Eventually we climb a hill, turning right and right again, bouncing over a rise and coming to a stop. Boots jumps out, leaving the engine running. Lanks wraps fingers around my shoulder, holding me in place. I hear the rumble of a garage door lifting. Boots climbs back in and we pull forward. He jumps back out and the rumble begins again, ceasing with a solid thud.

The hands holding me down let go. I pull myself upright. Lanks takes my arm and maneuvers me out of the truck and down off the running board.

The tape on my eyes has worked loose on the lower edge, as I step out of the truck, tiny sections of garage reveal themselves, one wall covered with a white sheet, around other walls, tools and benches. The room smells of fresh wood and new paint.

I force myself to remain upright despite the trembling, my thoughts wild. I cannot imagine what they're doing and can think only of a ransom attempt but struggle to figure out how they know that my stepfather has wealth.

Boots speaks for the first time since he ordered the blindfold, solemnly announcing, "It's all up to you."

I try keeping my voice casual. The mouse squeak I manage isn't what I hoped, "What is?"

He says nothing else but I can see the gun below the tape as he waves it under my chin. The gesture is lost on me. I bubble with panic. He jabs me in the side with the gun, pushing me toward the sheet-covered wall. Lanks, still gripping my arm, lifts the sheet and pushes me into the narrow passageway between it and the wall.

We travel a few feet behind the sheet towards the back of the garage until Boots commands, "Hold it." For good measure, he jabs me with the gun once more.

There is a trapdoor at my feet, and suddenly I know what they're doing: they're going to bury me alive. I'm stunned. The shock freezes my legs. Lanks keeps me upright.

I read about this in *Reader's Digest*, the crumpled one at the dentist's office. The story swarms back in full detail: the ransom attempt, the little girl, the hole underground, the coffin with the air tube that is too small, the hours she spent before she died. Only a tiny whimper seeps out, but my thundering heart is screaming at the universe.

Boots shifts the trapdoor cover and reveals a wooden ladder leading down into a short tunnel. He climbs down. Lanks lifts me up and dangles me over the hole. Boots pushes my feet onto a ladder rung and braces me against it while Lanks finishes lowering me down.

The passage below is walled and narrow. At the opposite end is a doorway. Boots pushes me down the hall and through the door, moving us into a more open space. I hear the thud of the trapdoor set back into place, before Lanks joins us in the small underground room.

Green utility carpet covers the floor beneath me. I see the edge of a low bench. This doesn't look like a burial pit. I teeter back; perhaps they aren't going to bury me. Maybe I'm mistaken. I thank whatever savior intervened.

"Sit." Boots orders again.

I sink awkwardly to the floor, my legs shaking too hard to support me on the way down, my arms useless still taped behind my back. I fall sideways, landing hard on my shoulder, the fall knocking a sharp breath from me.

I jerk upright to sit, yanking the damned tape still binding my wrists. My hands are icy. Struggling is useless, the tape won't give, but the effort comforts me. My voice returns.

"Get this off me!" I shriek, fighting the bindings.

Boots answers me in a low growl, "We'll take it off, then it's up to you." He reiterates, "All up to you."

He yanks the tape off the back of my head, taking a wad of hair with it. The tape peels from my eyes, leaving sticky bits that pin my eyes shut with each blink.

Finally, he begins unwrapping my wrists.

"I'm trusting you now…You got nothing to worry about." The pressure relaxes on my arms. "You keep sitting quiet, just like that. No reason we gotta hurt you."

The tape is off, but he keeps my arms gripped in place. "You understanding me?"

"I understand you, perfectly." I assume the nuance and venom are wasted.

He releases my arms. I pull them carefully around to my lap, both arms numb and shoulders burning from the long restraint. As feeling returns, with fingertips I worry at the bits of glue on my eyelashes and look more closely at the surroundings.

Bunk beds are built into one end of the room. An unframed mirror hangs over a freestanding cabinet along the wall in front of me. Behind me, a low wall heater runs the length of the room with a wooden slat bench in front of it. Pinned in neat rows on the otherwise bare walls are several years' worth of glossy, vulgar centerfolds.

My panic lessens a little with return of mobility and eyesight. My heart still slams in my chest, but I am no longer paralyzed. Now, I want to fight. This appears to be what the men expect, a run for the passageway. They watch me, poised to chase their prey.

I make no move. I summon insouciance. "Nice decorations." The sarcasm falls flat.

They smirk.

"So, what are we doing here?" I try to sound only marginally interested.

I don't truly want an answer to this. I want to sit, still and calm, me over here and the two of them over there, but I know my façade won't hold for very long. I need to know what's coming.

"You'll find out soon as the other guys get here." Lanks grins, his face curiously childlike, incongruous on his tall frame.

"Are my friends all right?" I realize I hadn't given them any thought since I was lifted from the VW bus. Now that they've come to mind, I'm a little hurt that they let me be stolen without a peep. I can't help but think our on-the-road code called for at least a small effort on my behalf. My concepts of liberation and chivalry openly clash.

Boots sneers, "Oh, yeah, your *friends*." He draws out the term. "They're fine."

"Where are they?"

"Shut up." The sneer becomes a bite; his sharp features contort, "Let's get you ready."

He approaches me and I avoid looking at his face. I'm about to find out what is happening here. I stop breathing and stare at the denim knees in front of me.

"This can be easy or real hard. We don't care which. You can't get out of here. You want to scream go ahead. Scream your pretty head off. Nobody's up there. This is a bomb shelter. The walls are two-feet thick."

He reaches over me and grabs my shirt on either side, pulling it off up over my head. I sit, naked from the waist up, bras having become socially optional, numb, paralyzed again. No reaction is appropriate for this. I can think of nothing to do. The two men stare; naughty boys getting away with a juicy bit.

Boots grabs my ankle, preparing to pull off my cowboy boot.

"Nice boots." He sounds impressed, lifting my leg higher and looking more closely.

They are nice, Frye, a birthday gift from a boyfriend's brother. I always suspected that he lifted them from Olsen Nolte's Saddlery where he worked at the time, though it seemed rude to make such an accusation. Now, I silently thank him for not giving me the Beatle boots I really wanted.

I grab at the compliment, clinging to this flicker of recognition of me as a person. Up to this moment, I've been anonymous. Now, I'm a girl who appreciates quality cowboy boots. Maybe he'll realize he has mistakenly kidnapped a kindred spirit. I try.

I smile, putting it into my voice. "Thanks, yeah, they're good boots. I've had them a long time."

He finally lowers my leg and pulls the boot off, continuing to admire it, smiling at me now, not with the disdainful smirk that preceded it, but the slimy smile of bar pickups. I have connected.

He doesn't stop what he's doing, but I feel infinitesimally reassured about what is coming, even though I'm still not sure what that will be. I'll be naked, apparently. My worst fear now is that they are going to torture me for fun. I prepare to talk them out of it.

My undresser pulls off the other boot. I let him unbutton my jeans and pull those off too, not helping, but not resisting. Once they're off, I sit in my underwear and watch him as he goes through the pockets, pulling out my wallet and the wad of bills I put there for safekeeping when I was worried that someone might steal it from the unattended van, the irony not lost on me.

He flashes the money to Lanks who is staring at me, slack-faced, entranced. I wonder if he has ever seen a naked girl before, except in glossy print.

Boots opens my wallet and reads my driver's license.

"Hawaii, huh? What are you doing here?"

What, indeed. I am not inclined to chat just now.

"Got lost."

He chuckles, "Yes, you did, honey."

He puts the wallet and money on the cabinet and returns to me, taking my wrist and pulling me to a stand. Again, I don't resist or help. I just do it. He grabs a leather thong that hangs over my head. I hadn't noticed it hanging there. Another hangs a foot or so away, both secured by ring bolts in the ceiling. He ties the thong to one wrist, then ties the other.

As he ties them, I decide the men are sadists, perhaps satanic worshipers. I assume they mean to torture me to death. I manage no reaction. What could possibly be appropriate? I am beyond my ability to think this through. It just can't be happening so reacting to it cannot possibly be necessary. And although I can no longer catch my breath, since I am no longer present, it isn't really necessary.

Boots stands in front of me and slowly, ritually, pulls my panties down my legs. He pauses, kneeling in front of me, his breath warming my crotch. Stale cigarette smoke wafts from him. Finally, he takes the panties off under my feet and tosses them on the pile with the rest of my clothing.

Next, he ties my ankles with thongs attached to bolts in the floor. I hadn't noticed these either. I am left dangling from the ceiling, spread-eagle, naked, forced to place weight on one set of tiptoes or the other, being stretched too tight to stand flat-footed on the floor. Hanging, I fight to catch my breath, my heart, along with my brain, having lost its mind.

The heat of their staring melts my numbness. Tears fall, running haphazardly across my cheeks and mouth. I wipe my face on my shoulders and struggle to stop gasping and crying, desperate they not see me frightened. I want this little victory.

The tears stop. I call on the adolescent brat. She is very strong. I rely on her conviction that she is the only person in the universe with any real intelligence, insufferable in a fourteen-year-old, vital right now.

"You guys are so weird."

They stop staring at me and exchange puzzled looks. Apparently, they're prepared for me to fight and cry, not to be rude.

Boots sits down on the bench behind me, inches away. My skin crawls, goose bumps race over my arms and legs, his acrid scent wrinkling my nose. I feel a breeze from a vent over me, warm like the room, but my body is chill.

"What exactly are we doing?" I do want an answer now.

"We're having some fun."

"This isn't fun. What are you're talking about?"

"She's not very smart," Lanks chimes in.

I splutter.

I'm not smart? You pull a gun on me and hang me from the ceiling, and I'm not very smart?"

In silence, I twirl a little, trying to relieve both indignation and the strain on my arms.

"Well, see, there's this old guy who lives here. We get him girls cuz he's too old to get 'em himself. He'll be here in a little while." Lanks guffaws at his scenario, as if this is a great joke.

I don't know if he's serious, but this sounds plausible, and compared to the sadistic torture I'm imaging, a little less horrible.

"What about the other two guys? You said we were waiting for them."

"They want to watch." Lanks cracks up again and drags knobby fingers through his stringy black hair.

"You guys are even weirder than I thought."

Banging wood in the hallway signals the arrival of the two others. My cockiness evaporates. Boots and Lanks have been less intimidating from the first. Lanks appears simpleminded, too stupid to know better. Boots is mercurial, but I have made a slight connection. I'm more frightened of the other two.

Red appears in the hall doorway, pausing a moment to survey the scene before strolling on in. The trapdoor thumps into place, and Thug too, ducks through into the room. They stand side by side and take long looks. Neither seems the slightest bit surprised to see me hanging naked in the center of the room.

Red's lips grimace to a frigid smile, "How about a drink?"

"Yeah!" Boots hurries over to the cabinet below the mirror and opens its door. With a flourish, he pulls out a bottle of rum and waves it around, gloating at the great treasure. Utah is a dry state, this contra-band another naughty toy.

The men appear to forget me, gathering around the makeshift bar. Boots opens a bottle of coke and puts a splash in four, red plastic cups. He finishes by filling each to the brim with rum. I dangle, dancing toe to toe, willing myself to keep breathing and to not be here now.

Each man takes a red cup from Boots as he finishes pouring. Lanks sips his drink, gagging with each swallow. Thug drains his in two quick gulps. Boots and Red savor theirs, as if appreciating fine wine.

"How about you, honey? Your turn." Boots mixes another and brings it over. He holds the plastic cup to my mouth and tries pouring the liquid in.

I shake my head, pulling away from the cup as best I can.

"Not my favorite. No, thanks."

"Not your favorite?" He sounds incredulous, brandishing the cup in front of my face, "This is the best rum money can buy."

I doubt that, more likely the only one. I refuse again.

"Come on. Relax." Red takes hold of the back of my hair and pulls my head back as far as it will go.

"Just a little sip." Boots tries again to pour it through my clamped lips.

I have never tasted hard liquor. As a teenager, I spent afternoons in Hawaii at the Shell and in San Francisco at Golden Gate Park drinking from huge bottles of Spanada wine being passed around by the crowds, but I have never even smelled rum. I know I'm going to throw up if any gets into my mouth. I yank my head forward trying to free my hair from Red's grip, knocking my face into the cup, splashing the drink down my neck and chest. Red jerks me back hard.

"Drink." He tries to hold my head still. My lips stay gripped shut tight.

Boots cuts off the battle. "Don't waste it on her."

Red gives my hair a final yank and lets go.

Boots stares at my face as he downs the remainder of the spilled drink. He seems puzzled, sizing me up. Lanks is excited by the confrontation, sipping his own drink as fast as he can.

Boots puts down the cup and opens the cupboard door once again. This time he brings out a bottle of rubbing alcohol and a pair of scissors. He soaks a small towel with the alcohol and comes over to me, leaving the scissors on the cabinet.

"Just a little precaution. Never know where you've been."

He lays the damp towel on my neck, the chill shocking me, sending goose bumps crawling up my arms, the scent carrying memories of childhood doctor visits.

Boots slowly slides the towel across my chest, fondling as he runs it over my breasts, continuing down across my belly and between my legs.

I keep my eyes locked on his, he watching for my reaction, me struggling to deny him any.

He probes with the damp towel, washing me thoroughly, smiling with some sense of personal triumph, crossing behind me to continue the intimate bath. The three other men watch every move. I lower my eyes to the floor and begin counting carpet fibers.

He finishes with a token sweep up my back before plunging once more between my legs. Then he takes the towel back to the cabinet, carefully folding and putting it away.

This time when he returns from the cabinet, he brandishes scissors. As he crosses the room, I imagine him stabbing me or slowly slicing me into pieces. My relief at an easier fate evaporates. But why I have to be clean for this isn't making sense.

However, instead of random slices, he picks up a section of hair and pulls it away from my head, preparing to cut it off at the scalp.

"NO! NO!" I roar. This cruelty scares me awake. I jerk back, tossing my head every direction. He holds tight. The leather thongs wrapped around my wrists and ankles give nothing. Hanging, a fly in a web, I thrash uselessly.

"I don't have lice. God, no, don't cut off my hair, no, please." Somehow neither guns nor nudity have scared me this much. "I'm not dirty. I've only been traveling a few days. You don't have to cut my hair." Despair taking over, I sob.

My wrists and ankles are raw from twisting against the bindings, blood drips from a healing burn on my arm, a parting wound from my final coffee pot at work. I stop struggling.

Boots holds the scissors before my face and surveys the room. Red sneers. Thug shrugs it off, palms up. Lanks grins.

"Okay." He lets go of the hair, smoothing it back into place.

"Shame to cut off such pretty hair." He smiles at me again as if flirting with a bar pickup. The scissors are put back into the cabinet.

I relax. Apparently my fear of being cut to pieces is too abstract for hysteria, but a bad haircut, to this I can relate.

CHAPTER 3

Experienced

The small success encourages me. "Please take these off." I shake my arms as best I can. "I can't stand like this anymore."

The mood in the room changes abruptly. Suddenly, the men are in motion. Thug kneels down and begins untying the leather thongs binding my ankles. He doesn't speak or look directly at me while he works the knots.

"This can go real easy for you. You just enjoy yourself, and we'll all have a good time." Boots, hyped up now, admonishes me once more as I'm released.

With my ankles freed, I bring each foot in underneath me to take the pressure off my hands and arms. My legs are shaking, but it's better than balancing on my toes. I savor the improvement. My arms, finally released, fall heavily to my sides, numb, one shoulder refusing to hang properly. Thug backs off, and I drop to the rough carpet, gathering my naked self into its own small space. Still not certain what they intend, but not encouraged by their promise that it doesn't have to be horrible, I huddle on the floor and try my best to disappear.

Boots adjusts a switch by the door. We go dark, then my eyes adjust and the room re-emerges, all of us now bathed in hellish, red lighting.

"Take off your clothes." Boots barks orders to the others.

Curled in a ball, I watch them spread out around the room as they begin to undress. They unlace work boots, pull off sweaty socks, unbutton cowboy shirts, and strip off T's. Clothes pile up on the beds, floor, bench. Belts rattle as they're unbuckled. Jeans are unbuttoned and pushed to the floor to be stepped from, boxers and jocks dragged down and off, their acrid scents blending and clashing in the small room.

I am astonished. I can't believe four grown men will strip naked in front of each other with such ease. I'm embarrassed for them, huddled here in my tiny hiding place on the floor.

The four, each naked now, gather around me. I try being smaller. From my perspective, they tower over me, a forest of hairy, white legs in a haze of florid lighting.

"Okay," Boots begins, "Why don't you come lie down over here?"

I don't move or respond to his demand, so he rolls and swings me to the center of the room, then pushes my shoulders back to lay me down.

I'm frozen again. This will be rape, I decide. I'm not to be buried alive nor cut to pieces. I am a little relieved, actually, given the alternatives I've imagined, and I bless Planned Parenthood for my birth control pills, the horror of potential pregnancy avoided, but I am puzzled. What drives men to this? Why the drama, the gun, the tethers? What makes this necessary or appealing? I find no response beyond the thought appropriate. I give none.

Boots slips a clammy foot between my legs, edging them apart. Then, kneeling down, he grips my ankles and spreads them a little farther. Trying to avoid looking at his face, I stare up at the other three above me. Each grips his own penis, hands jerking spastically up and down, stroking and watching.

Boots holds a tube of KY jelly. He smears a glob on himself then squeezes more onto his fingers and wipes them onto me, intruding, exploring.

Snaking up between my legs, he stretches out on top of me, trying to kiss me, one hand catching my face, the other guiding himself into me. I struggle more to avoid the kiss than the penetration. He loses interest in forcing my cooperation as he's caught in his own pleasure, his bony hips jabbing my belly as he rams himself into me.

"Move your hips. Men like that," his sex advice delivered as a husky command.

Sure, buddy.

I lift a little.

"More. Really move them."

I have been trying to remain as flat on the floor as I can, hiding under him out of sight of our audience, pretending I am not here at all. Now, he reaches around and lifts each thigh, pulling my knees up and wide apart around him.

I turn my head as far as it will go to avoid seeing the ghouls standing over me, still jerking off in their absurd red nakedness. I close my eyes and remember a gorgeous tabby cat we had when I was a child. He would sit on a kitchen chair and close his eyes, then reach up slowly with one gigantic paw and search the table with it until he found a bit of food he could carefully pull off onto the chair. I knew that he assumed if his eyes were closed, we couldn't see him. I lie there with the carpet scraping skin off my back, Boots humping away, and hope he was right. Tears fall.

Boots rams into me in a final spasm, pulling out and standing up as soon as the last shudder passes, a satisfied bantam rooster. He swaggers to the cabinet for the towel.

Without discussion, Lanks smears jelly on himself and lies down on me to take his turn.

"Don't cry," his voice full of concern. "You like this."

His skin smooth and hot, he slips easily between my legs.

I keep my head turned away and don't speak, wondering if he believes what he said, the innocence and malevolence belonging in two different people.

He moans and comes quickly, too excited after watching and jerking off to take long. He relaxes, sprawling, his legs and arms covering me.

"Hey man, get off the bitch." Red kicks Lank's thigh. Lanks pushes himself up and hangs poised over me.

"You feel real good." He pushes back on his haunches and stands.

My screamed rebuttal fades to a silent whisper, "*How can you do this?*"

Red kneels between my legs. He puts his hands on my bent knees, spreading them, trying his best to force each down to the carpet. I'm not that limber. He watches my face as he pushes them to their limit, showing his teeth when I grimace from the pain.

"I want a lot of action, honey."

His body is enormous, cascading in expanding rolls from his chin to his groin, genitals hidden under folds of fat. He is going to squash me flat. I know it. I take a deep breath, preparing for the burden as he lowers his bulk down onto me.

I'm fascinated; the fat has no substance. It flows onto me like liquefied Jell-O, spilling over my sides to the floor. At its center, a scrawny frame comes to rest on top of me. He doesn't watch. He closes his eyes and concentrates on his own motion.

I make a few small lifts to avoid a demand for more. He grunts and seems to be working hard. I suspect his personal pleasures run to the more complex.

Boots and Lanks sit on the bench, watching and exchanging comments I can't hear, Lanks now wiping off with the towel. Thug still stands over me, slowly stroking himself.

My back stings, rubbed raw already by the rough carpet. Red takes longer than the first two, sweat soon dripping off his chest into my eyes. Through the blur, red rays from the overhead lights sparkle and spread in all directions. I watch them, just them.

Red works up to frantic thrusting, crashing into my pubic bone. I wiggle a bit, hoping to hurry him along. He finally spasms and holds the final thrust, relaxing only a moment before pulling off me, leaving me soaked in his sweat.

"Whew, baby." He chortles as he stands up.

I'm so glad he's pleased. I hope he has a heart attack.

He grabs the towel from Lanks, who has just used it to wipe his own genitals, and wipes his face with it.

I lift up on my elbows to soothe my burning back.

"Not yet," Thug growls at me.

I lie back down.

He lays his solid, hairy body on top of me and pushes into me hard. Unlike the others, he does watch me, moving his hips but not his eyes. His pace is steady, unhurried even as he comes. His eyes never leave mine. In them, I see the only man here who understands this is a crime.

He takes a deep breath before pulling off of me and standing up. Now, I have been raped.

Finished with their first round, the men are done with me for the moment, occupied among themselves. I lie in a sticky puddle. My back no longer stings, it's numb. My whole body trembles, freezing and sweating. I turn onto my side and fold up. I close my eyes and wish again that I could disappear or simply find somewhere to hide. I wish I had Grammy's big green chair.

Grammy lives in San Diego in a modest house high on a ridge. Her sidewalks shimmer in the heat. When we're young, Big Sis and I stay with her while Mom teaches dance in Palo Alto. I practice my tap steps—out back down, out back down, step together, step together, out back down—on the porch while I wait for her to come for us.

The house is stucco with a red-painted concrete porch bounded by iron railings. The iron swirls leave just enough space for my head and arms to slip through. When I'm tired of practicing, I hang there in the shaded heat, staring at the still houses across the avenue and wish my mom would come back to get me.

By the time I'm a presence in his home, Grandpa is a drunk, a true alcoholic. One sip of liquor and he is lost. His eyes, his posture, the timbre of his voice, all give him away. Most evenings when he comes in from his garage, the screen-door slam signals angry voices and stern warnings will follow.

My grandparents also have a boarder. She is frail and smells of old age. Her snow-white hair pulled up in a tight bun bristles with silver bobby pins. She appears to be made of parchment. I'm afraid of her.

Each evening, she shuffles into the living room from the second bedroom, a tiny corner room that is also a hallway from the bathroom to the kitchen porch (I blame the sweet suffocating scent of the bathroom on her), settles herself carefully into the rocking chair that envelopes her tiny frame, straightens her shawl, and stares at me. She calls me "special." I find this ominous.

To avoid her eyes and Grandpa's temper, I hide behind the giant, green-upholstered armchair where Grammy sits. While seated in it, she embroiders infinitesimal designs on napkins and placemats, or plays Scrabble with Sis. From behind the chair, I listen to Grammy brush aside Grandpa's drunken belligerence, and I avoid the boarder's piercing stare.

Across the room, the TV plays grown-up shows, Ed Sullivan in black and white, Walter Winchell explaining troubles. I sit behind the chair and sort buttons from the button box.

The box holds a lifetime of extra buttons, some sparkly, some tiny, most blue or brown or black. I sort, put back, search for the special sparkly button. Sometimes, it's right there. Sometimes, I can't find it.

But there is no big green chair here. I doubt now that I'll see Grammy or the button box again. I curl up more tightly, clutching my shaking legs close.

Someone has turned on the radio. I wonder if it's been on all along and I just haven't noticed. George Harrison sings gently to his Lord. This is prayer I understand. I join him for the chorus and my trembling eases.

The men ignore me. They sit or wander around the room, bathed in the red haze, naked, flaccid, sipping more rum and coke. I think about Jesus.

Boots reappears next to me. He is jerking off frantically. "Turn over."

It will be doggy-style this time. I don't have to look at them. My back to them, no eyes, no faces, this has nothing to do with me. The radio plays. I hum with Janis, me and Bobby, lost here together.

Boots, Lanks, and Thug take turns. My insides are bruised, I ignore them. The rhythmic pain has a life of its own, surging and receding as they pound away. They each work hard to come a second time. I assume they're trying to impress one another. I think Boots fakes it.

"Freedom's just another word..." I hum along.

Red chooses sodomy for his second turn. The pain rips me back. I can't stand it. I have cooperated from the beginning. I have been a docile coward to avoid giving them reason to follow through on the threats, but I can't stand this; this makes me furious.

"Stop it!" I scream full on.

His manicured fingernails dig into my hips, he jabs away. I'm shrill, in agony, "Stop it!"

To my surprise, Boots issues another command, "Let her go."

I am right about him; he's connected.

Red takes a few final stabs and then shoves me away. "All right, bitch."

I have been braced on all fours, three really—one arm won't support anything—and now I sink back onto my folded legs, huddling in a lump, hoping I no longer appear human.

Boots, Thug, and Red light cigarettes, the room fills with smoke. I think of my mother, her scarlet lips always clenching a lit cigarette. I wish I had said goodbye to her. I don't expect to see her again. I assume they'll kill me, and I begin to hope it will be soon. I don't think I can do this much longer.

Lanks steps up and looms over me. Leaning down, he unfolds me and lays me again on my back. The raw skin on my back burns. He lays himself on top of me, propped on his elbows, resting casually, staring at my face.

"I don't smoke. I don't." His voice and eyes are pleading, earnest.

I can't imagine why this matters. "Okay."

"I don't. I don't smoke."

"Okay, fine."

"You believe me?"

"Sure. Yeah. Why would you lie?" The absurdity overwhelms me. I choke on a giggle, part hysteria, part genuine amusement.

You're a kidnapper and rapist, but you're worried that I'll think you're a smoker?

I don't say anything more. I take a few breaths and wait.

He seems satisfied. "Now, it's your turn." He begins slithering down my stomach. "You're gonna like this."

His intention knocks my breath out. The giggle twists to gasp.

His face hovers over my crotch, "I'm gonna make you come."

He can't possibly mean to do this. I have to die right now.

My voice gives away nothing, "No, you aren't. I'd have to be enjoying myself, and I definitely am not." I spit venom with this last, mixed with hot panic.

I have no idea if this is true; how much is under my control is a mystery. My reputation far exceeds my experience. But I can't be wrong. I just can't be, not right now.

"Girls really like this." He is an idiot. My façade holds.

"No one would enjoy it under these circumstances." I clench my jaw and stare at him.

He hesitates, apparently confused. He seems to be wondering who lied to him. His hands stop their efforts and he backs away. I am spared this particular humiliation. I hold my breath and stare at him until he is entirely away. Behind the stare, I am still trying my best to disappear.

Thug picks up his boxers and steps into them. Red follows suit. I'm thankful, but continue trying to vanish.

Static bubbles from speakers near the cabinet. Boots jumps up and goes to it. He adjusts dials on the cabinet surface. Male voices come through speakers.

"Hey man, what's up?"

Boots motions silence to all of us in the room. He looks at me a long time before responding, "Hey, nothing, nothing. Can't come up right now."

"How about us coming down?"

Boots hesitates again before he answers, "Can't tonight, man, not tonight. Later, okay?"

Voices in the background grumble a little. "Okay. Later."

The speaker static quits.

Boots switches it off and turns to me. "You're real lucky." He looks for appreciation, "I could've invited them down."

I am to be grateful for the favor.

"Yeah, you would've really liked them." Lanks emphasizes the "really." He too seems to think I'm lucky it's only these four. The others grunt their agreement.

I play it. "Thanks." The very heart of sincerity.

"You're welcome."

I understand I have dodged something else. I don't want to imagine now what they think would be worse, although I assume satanic worship and death-by-burial are still on the table.

"Need to use the john?"

I do, desperately. I need to drown myself.

Thug motions for me to follow him into the hallway where a bucket with a makeshift toilet seat across it now sits in front of the ladder. He stands in the doorway and watches me sit, not taking his eyes off me as I relieve myself.

I sit as long as I can. No one is touching me, only watching. I imagine my escape: scrambling up the ladder, hurling aside the trapdoor, racing through the garage screaming, screaming. I expect that once begun, the screams won't stop.

I check Thug. He's reading my thoughts. I put them aside. I won't get one rung up the ladder.

I get up and brush past him back into the den.

Boots waves a Polaroid camera at me.

"Let's get some pictures. You get over there."

He motions me to the wall with the pinups strewn across it.

"How about on your knees, real flashy."

I pose and re-pose, letting him adjust me this way and that. Lanks hoots and twitters as the flash erupts over and over in my face. The others grab the ejected photos and hover over them as the lewd images resolve, guffawing and crooning as they pass the pictures around. The poses get raunchier.

I will my heart to stop beating. I try holding my breath long enough to lapse into unconsciousness. I beg for insanity. I demand to be released from awareness.

I get absolutely no cooperation from my Self. I see every leer. I feel every touch, every ache in my exhausted body. I remain cursedly present.

The photo shoot ends. The men sprawl around, smoking and slobbering over the pictures. I sink again into a small space, closing my eyes and hiding in the radio's lyrics of love and freedom—lies.

The men's voices intrude.

"What time is it?"

"Midnight."

I open my eyes; it's my twentieth birthday.

"We're going to get something to eat. You want something, honey?" Red, pulling on his jeans, manages to make this snide.

"Sort of a Last Supper?" Lanks looks to the others to see if his joke is funny. He, too, is dressing.

"We'll get Chinese."

I'm surprised there is a Chinese restaurant here in nowhere, and that it will be open at midnight, it might have been a good clue, though I don't think I'll need any now. I assume they're going to kill me, they can't be expecting to get away with this, and as much as I want to die this very moment, I desperately don't really want to.

"Don't do anything I wouldn't do." Red offers this parting hilarity before he, Thug, and Lanks jostle through the doorway. The thud of the trapdoor pushed aside and their boots on the ladder reverberates through the little room. Boots sits on the lower bunk bed, still naked, smoking a cigarette.

He crushes it in an overflowing tin ashtray on the cabinet and holds out a hand to me. I stare at the outstretched hand, nicotine-stained fingers and bitten nails.

"Come over here."

I try to shake my head but can only think about moving. My muscles have seized and nothing moves on the outside, although my insides quiver uncontrollably.

"I want you over here," his weasel face narrows, "now." He whines this angry demand.

One arm is useless. With the other, I lift my legs to straighten them, groaning involuntarily as I do.

"You sore? I can fix that."

Am I sore?

I wish I had the strength to kill him or even just to spit at him, but I don't, I'm drifting away.

He moves to my end of the room, kneels down beside me, and begins kneading my outstretched thighs. Bile rises into my throat.

"Feel better?"

I nod, hoping he'll stop.

He switches to stroking my hair.

"You're really pretty." He takes my hand and puts it on him, making me stroke him as he gets another erection. He continues smoothing my hair.

Laying me down, he climbs on again. This time he wraps his arms around me and holds me like a lover, kissing my neck and trying again to kiss my mouth, an incongruous version of tender desire distorting his face. I strain to keep my face out of reach.

He twines around me, whispering obscene sweet nothings. The air has cooled; his body is clammy and I'm chilled, my rug-burns howling as he runs his hands up and down my raw back.

I realize he is acting out his fantasy of romantic love, pretending I'm here voluntarily. I let him pretend, my revulsion pulsing behind what I hope is an impassive face. I become an excellent prostitute. The hookers who looked after me in Denver make sense now, distance is their saving grace.

Before he's quite finished, the trapdoor bangs again, bringing an abrupt end to his fantasy. He pushes away and jumps up as the others return.

CHAPTER 4

Devil's Sympathy

The other three men lumber in, small white boxes with thin wire handles dangling from their fingers. The sweet scent of ginger fills the room. I scoot backwards to the wall, draw my legs close, and watch the men arrange themselves for dinner. I fight the trembling, shivers rattle my teeth. I can't breathe. I huddle tight, holding onto Me.

"Sure you aren't hungry? There's plenty." Ever the gracious host, Boots pulls on his shorts before chowing down.

I whisper, "No."

The men chat about a friend's new truck, his wife didn't approve, another is moving to Montana. They smack and chew. Someone smokes.

I try praying; what the hell.

The night before, at the motel where we took refuge, I read through the Gospels. I have context and terminology, if not faith. I think of a woman I met in Hawaii, a bag lady in the parking lot of the Ala Moana Shopping Center who promised me Jesus would save me whenever I was in need. I believe I am at the moment, although what might be done about it now eludes me.

"Dear God…," in silence I compose prayers. I close my eyes and lose myself in their composition, appreciating archaic phrasing juxtaposed with hysteria. My breath slows. I stop shivering and open my eyes.

The men are finishing their meal. Greasy, crumpled containers get tossed in a pile beside the cabinet. Boots reclines on the lower bunk and lights another cigarette. Red perches on the edge beside him. Thug and Lanks share the bench.

"You guys do this often?" I find my voice, calm enough now to be sarcastic.

The men exchange quizzical looks, Red finally assuming the role of spokesman.

"Actually, you are the first, but it's gonna be a great summer." He laughs from the belly up.

I am incredulous, "How can you expect to get away with this?"

Red puffs up, "Let's just say we have...protection."

Boots shoots him a glance.

"What protection?" I ask in as snide a tone as I can manage.

"Well, see...I'm a lawyer and I take care of my friends." He is still puffed up, full beach ball. I assume he's lying, but I don't know any lawyers; he might be telling the truth.

I can't interpret the looks the men exchange. They seem to be reassuring each other that this conversation hasn't gone too far. Thug's jaw knots. Boots glowers at him.

The discussion leaves me wondering if killing me is not the plan after all, since they're now worrying about what I know.

Lanks appears unconcerned, "Yeah, Red's gotta be in court in the morning."

They all chuckle. I wonder on which side of the bench he's scheduled to appear, but I can't tell whether they're laughing at my gullibility or the delicious irony of the truth. I hold my disdainful veneer.

"Sure, of course." I drip contempt, but I'm not sure. This could explain the boldness of the kidnapping, driving off with me in broad daylight from a public place.

"You don't seem too scared." Boots gets off the bed and comes to stand over me where I am folded, my back against the wall.

I watch him, but avoid looking at his eyes; they're dark.

"Let's see how scared you really are." He puts one hand around my throat and pulls me to a stand. "We work for..."

I'm not sure what he says next. Whatever it is, it means nothing to me.

"We make gyroscopes."

Is this supposed to frighten me? Is this pertinent?

Once again, I'm at a complete loss. I remain motionless, pinned against the wall, his hand on my throat.

Apparently, a blank look is not what he's pushing for. He grips my neck with the other hand and his fingers tighten. I meet his eyes and hold them. A madman stares back. I wrap my fingers around his wrists. Flashes of light burst in my eyes and I need to breathe. I begin tugging, uselessly, at his arms.

He lifts me off the ground. My legs dangle, then kick, panic torturing my lungs. I can't see him clearly, then he fades into the distance beyond swirling dark. I claw and kick, but my hands are lost, my legs are lost, the room is lost.

When the world swirls back, I can see me, a tiny me, lying in a corner far away, just visible in near darkness. I'm crying.

The real Me is way up high, floating in a warm golden bubble. It's quiet and still, and I'm not alone. A golden man stands behind me. Below, in the distance, I can see the men moving about. They are naked again.

Boots' weasel face looms at me, distorted, elongated as through a doorway peephole, all mouth, then nose, then eyes.

"Time for some more fun." The voice blares into my face. The face down there, up here, nowhere.

He stands close, rubbing himself hard. He grabs the tiny figure's face and shoves himself into her mouth.

I gag. He grips my hair, holding me kneeling, slamming his bony crotch against my lips, forcing himself farther and farther down my throat. I choke, letting spittle and salty liquid dribble down my chin. He releases me and steps away.

Before I sink down, Thug grabs my hair and pushes himself in, jerking my head back hard as my teeth scrape flesh. Fetid pubic hair envelopes my face. I gasp in pain as he rams himself down my bruised throat until he's done. I struggle not to swallow, and finally released, I spit what I can onto the floor.

Red steps up. The muscles in my jaw spasm as he pries my lips apart with his finger and slides himself inside.

"Don't think about biting me, bitch."

I think of nothing. He is easier, too small to reach my throat. I have only to keep my teeth from the bite he worries about. The muscles in my legs struggle to hold me up. My jaw is on fire. He comes, and I add to the puddle I kneel in.

Lanks wraps his fingers roughly in my hair, pressing my face against him. He drives himself into my mouth, down my throat. I choke and gag, vomit swirling up into my mouth. I brace my hands against his thighs and push, fighting to pull my head back enough to catch my breath and spit, but I'm trapped against the wall. He clamps me more firmly to him, ramming himself insistently down my throat.

Suffocating on my own vomit, I try harder to push him away, tearing at his legs, but I have no strength left. Spongy all over, I gain nothing. His grip tightens around my head, my eyes burn from sweat dripping off his belly. He arches and grunts. Salty goo sprays down my throat. My face pressed so solidly against him I have no choice, strangling and whimpering, I swallow vomit and semen.

His fingers uncurl. I sink to the floor and float back to the ceiling.

I watch from high above, safe in my gold cocoon. The men move about, far off in a distant corner. Muffled voices drift up to Me. Boots brings out the camera once again.

Far away, a tiny me kneels on all fours, angry abrasions marring back and hips. This time they use me in pairs: one man behind, one in front, one taking photographs. They cycle around, taking turns as photographer, rapist, voyeur, passing around the emerging photos, braying at their cleverness.

Up here, I am warm, loved. The golden man and I drift. The naked men never touch Me.

The men sprawl around the room, smoking, taking turns going down the hall. Cigarette smoke spirals in the red glare below Me. The lost me sits slumped where the men have left her, staring at the floor.

"What time is it?" Thug's rumble reverberates up to Me.

Lanks finds a clock, "5:20."

"I gotta get ready for work."

"Yeah, me too."

"Gotta get rid of her."

"Yeah."

The four begin to dress—shorts, socks, pants. Shirts tucked in. Belt buckles clapped shut. They sit to tug on boots and heavy shoes. Hair combs slip from back pockets. They jockey for position in front of the small cabinet mirror. Red coaxes a few tendrils across his bald spot. Lanks drags knobby fingers through greasy black strands. Boots carefully parts and smoothes. Thug doesn't bother.

"Time to go. Get dressed." Boots drops my clothes in front of me. "Gotta get to work." His voice echoes.

I have no strength to pull air in or to let it out. I have no interest in it either. My arms and legs are distant. My insides vibrate. I don't know why I'm sitting here.

But he told me to get dressed. The sound of the words swirls in my head, and their meanings coalesce: I am to get dressed.

I coax my good arm to extend, to reach for my underwear, hesitating before picking them up, sure that I misunderstood, or that he will change his mind. He says nothing. I grip the panties and drag them up my legs without standing. I repeat the slow retrieval for my faded T-shirt and let it drop over my head.

The men are quiet. They loom over me, faces impassive. I stagger to my feet to pull on my jeans, rocking on jelly legs. The twirling room has trouble holding still. The jeans drag through the sweat and slime, over raw skin. I don't feel it.

Boots retrieves my Frye boots from under the bunk bed. He holds them up before handing them to me. "Really great boots."

I take them from him and sit down on the bench. I haven't enough strength to pull the boots on. Struggling to get my foot inside the first one, frustration and rage well up. I shove harder, and my foot plunges down. With all the strength left to me, I ram my foot into the second boot and stand up to face the end of this night.

I look around the room and stare for a moment at each man. Lanks won't meet my eyes, he looks to Thug. Thug will stare as long as I like. He sees me dead. Red smirks and turns away. I suppose for him, the best part is still ahead. Boots shifts from my eyes to my feet and back. He grabs my arm and turns me away.

I hear tape unraveling. He wraps a piece around my head, across my eyes. Once again my wrists are bound behind my back.

"You got the gun?" Thug growls the question.

Seconds pass in silence. Finally, Boots barks an answer, "No, it's in the cabinet."

"I'll get it." I hear the cabinet door click open, then closed.

"Okay, let's go." Boot's fingers close around my shoulder as he steers me through the hallway to the ladder. One of the men clambers up ahead of me and moves the trapdoor.

"Climb up. I'll keep you from falling." Boots braces a hand against my back. His touch burns. I understand the concern isn't for my welfare on the ladder, it's expediency—they're late for work.

From a far place, I watch my leaden-self climb the ladder. Each step takes total concentration. I gather bits of will to force each leg, lift, push, lift, push, out back down, out back down, step together, step together, out back down. What is left of me climbing this ladder wants to get out. She wants her life to end outside, under open sky.

I reach the top and suffer help from unseen hands to keep my balance. We retrace our steps behind the curtained wall. Stepping out into the garage, the cool fresh air is both shock and blessing. Escape doesn't cross my mind, dying does.

Boots guides me to the truck and opens the door, boosting me in. The garage door squeals open. Boots climbs in and the truck roars awake. He puts his hand on the back of my head and crumples me into my own lap, out of sight. I stink now too, but the warmth and darkness aren't unwelcome.

We back out of the driveway slowly. This time Thug rides with us. The garage door slams shut and he jumps in, overwhelming my small space, the heat of him sending me away. Boots lifts his hand off the back of my head, but I don't consider sitting up.

Very little of me rides in the pickup, most of me remains back in the pit, still naked on the floor in a pool of vomit, sweat and semen. The rest floats far above this truck, watching its meaningless progress.

We drive awhile on paved road, before turning off and driving on dirt roads for a time. I wonder if they'll kill me, then go home and shower, or just go straight to work.

Hours ago, when Boots mentioned an employer, he seemed to believe the revelation was going to frighten or enlighten me. I lost consciousness wondering which it was. A bit later, when I came to, it didn't seem important. Now, I'm curious as I ride curled into my own lap, humming along with the radio, "Joy to the world, all the boys and girls…" and drifting far above in my own small space.

We turn off the dirt road and come to a stop. Thug takes my arm and lifts me out. The sun is already warm. I hear the whine of the VW engine pull in beside us and shut off.

"May I have the blindfold off?" The sound of my voice surprises me. I didn't know I was asking a question. Now that I've spoken, I do want to see the world, even if it is scorched desert. I want a vision of sky and earth.

"I guess so." Thug pulls off the tape, almost gently.

We stand in an industrial parking lot in the midst of sprawling desert, at the dawn of a clear morning. Huge storage tanks loom in front of us. I see no other structures. The lot is deserted.

"Over here." Thug grabs my arm and pulls me to the lot's edge, then yanks me to a stop and pushes on my shoulder, forcing me to my knees.

I am glad it's almost over. Breathing takes too much effort, my trembling nears convulsion. The slamming of my own heart drums other sounds to whispers. I focus on the dust at my feet. A small, white flower stares back. It's my birthday. My mother will never know what happened to me. I wish I'd said goodbye before driving away. Tears overflow, splashing on the tiny flower.

Behind me, the men are arguing.

Thug shifts around and I feel the barrel of the gun press against the back of my head. He keeps his hand on my shoulder.

"No one will believe her. She's just a hippie." Boots' voice is clear. The responses overlap. I can't sort it out. I am preoccupied once more with not being here now.

I stop breathing. I demand my heart stop, but it refuses, pounding out lifetimes, the rest of my life, the end of my life.

"Wait up," Boots barks.

I drift in crystalline sky. I listen to Thug's raspy breath. He presses the gun a little harder into my head.

"What?" Thug barks, the strain telling in his voice.

"We think, maybe, we don't have to do that."

"What the fuck are you talking about?"

The gun metal drills into a spot behind my left eye. I can see it from where I am.

"Who's gonna believe her?" Boots repeats his dismissal of my ultimate credibility.

"Let her go." He wavers between command and question.

An eternity drifts by, the sun warm, the sky flawless. From far away, I watch me kneeling in the dust.

"Let her go." This time he does command, although I am too far away to care right this moment.

Another forever comes and goes.

Finally, as each has done all night, Thug obeys him. "Okay." He pulls the gun away and the pressure of his hand lifts from my shoulder.

Boots and Lanks confer in hushed voices. Thug moves to stand with Red.

"Come on." Lanks approaches and wraps his knobby fingers around my arm, helping me to stand, then unwraps the tape from my wrists. "We'll take you back."

Red and Thug exchange words with the others, then head to the VW bus and drive away. Their workday begins.

Lanks holds onto me and leads me to the pickup. As my world shifts between exaggerated and non-existent, I have trouble maneuvering.

We leave the parking lot, driving out into the desert opposite our entry, cutting through densely planted fields before returning to open desert. We ride in silence, sitting pressed together like old friends, pink dawn caressing the horizon in front of us.

Boots stops the truck in the middle of the dirt road. Other than this road, there is nothing.

"You get out here. Get out and don't turn around until you count to 100. Then just walk a couple more miles."

Not turn around? You think I'm going to memorize your license plate or throw rocks?

I should feel something, but none of this can be real or of any consequence. I move without my own help. I get out and stand beside the door before Lanks swings it closed.

I want to say something, something cutting and cruel and oh-so-clever, the definitive Last Word.

"God bless you. You really need it," blurts out instead. It isn't at all what I had in mind.

Boots hollers, "Don't turn around," revs the engine, and roars off.

I turn around immediately and watch them disappear in the billowing dusty haze. I try to memorize the plate, but it drifts away with the dust.

When the pickup is completely out of sight, I begin walking, one foot, the other, out back down, out back down, repeat, repeat. I move oblivious to the ground I cover or of the time that passes. The morning sun doesn't warm me. I hear nothing. Out back down, out back down, step together, step together.

I doubt I will ever arrive anywhere. I'm not sure I actually am anywhere now. Out back down, out back down. The outline of the world spins as the horizon tilts and lifts itself up to meet me.

I come to, bathed in sunlight, the desert quiet in its morning heat, my face resting in soft, warm dirt. I lie still. This will do. I'm never leaving here.

I sneeze, and clouds of dust sting my eyes, forcing me to sit up.

The fog evaporates, and I remember why I'm sitting here: I'm supposed to be walking. I am supposed to be walking back to my real life although I can't imagine who will live in it now.

My heart races again as panic wells up. Suddenly, I have to find cover. I can't be so exposed. I can't be in the open. I struggle to stand, all of me aching and weak, one arm hanging useless. I use the other to push myself off the ground.

Once standing, I can't remember which direction I'm supposed to be heading, if any. I make a guess from tracks in the dust and begin where they left off, one foot, the other, my legs stiff and uncooperative. Out back down, out back down.

The outhouse is the first building I see; the dirt road has led me to the back of the filling station. I try running, but my legs won't move any faster than the stiff straddle-step my exhausted muscles and swollen flesh allow. I'm desperate to reach the tiny shack before anyone sees me. No one can ever see me again.

I finally reach the shack and leap inside, fumbling in the sudden darkness to fasten the rusty latch, then crouching to the floor, curling again into as small a space as I'm able. I plan to stay alone here in the darkness until I die.

The night is ground into me. I already know clothing will never hide it, scrubbing never remove it, that I will always be naked and rank. Huddling tight, shivering and sweating simultaneously, I'm sick that they didn't shoot me.

I drift in and out, dreaming of claws, tendrils, suffocation. I wake to muscle cramps and reality. Dread soaks me, but I accept that I can't hide in here any longer. As unfathomable as it seems, I understand that life is going on outside.

Standing takes concentration; I'm frozen in place. I brace my good hand on the splintering wall plank and force myself to unfold. Finally upright, I fumble with the latch until it gives, and I slowly push open the door.

The sunlight blinds me. I stand frozen in place, spasms running up and down my back, my skin crusted with the night's cruelty. As sight resolves in the glaring daylight, and the spasms lessen, I understand that first I have to call the police, and then I have to go back to Hawaii. I am twenty years old and still alive.

CHAPTER 5

Uneven Streets

Reluctantly, I leave the safety of my tiny shelter and hobble to the station front. K sees me first. He leaps out the van's side door and runs to me.

"God, what happened? Where have you been? You look really bad." He frets and fusses.

Thanks. I'm not sure what happened, and I may feel worse than I look.

"I have to call the police." This is all I can get out.

"What happened?"

I ignore him. "I need a phone. Is there one? Can I borrow a dime?"

Guiding me to the edge of the open van door, he encourages me to sit. He looks rumpled from sleep. I lower myself to perch carefully on the door ledge. K tells me he and J were driven into the mountains and left tied up on the side of the road. After working themselves loose, they flagged down a car that returned them here.

"We called the sheriff, but they said there wasn't anything they could do about it until you showed up."

Until I showed up?

J climbs out of his sleeping bag, yawning and brushing silky bangs out of his eyes, "What happened?"

I can only mumble a non-answer. "They…they…"

"Well, at least you didn't have to give them blow jobs," he pipes in, seeming chipper about the whole thing.

I don't know why he thinks this. His bald comment strikes me—I loathe him for it. He is so wrong—and it makes me wonder if these two boys sold me, maybe with a condition on the amount of abuse the rapists were allowed to impose, or if perhaps they themselves were assaulted by Red and Thug, before being left on the road. I can't believe the first could be true. The very thought means I have no friends left at all, but neither boy offers anything further about their own possible nightmare and I don't ask.

"Lie down. I'll call the sheriff and tell him you're back. See what they want to do now."

K leaves me and heads towards the telephone booth out on the edge of the highway. I climb onto the bed in the back of the van and fall asleep despite the stifling heat inside.

K touches me lightly. I jerk awake and struggle away from the touch, shouting and fighting off the fog.

"The sheriff said you can call them if you want."

"If I want?" This takes time to make sense. "They aren't coming?"

"No, they said there isn't anything they can do, but you can call them, if you want." He drops the last part.

They can't come out to look for witnesses at the café? They can't ask about the VW bus that sticks out like a sore thumb among the pickup trucks? They can't find a Chinese restaurant that's open at midnight?

I get it. The sons-of-bitches were right. They know their turf. I am "just a hippie," less than human and still alive because of it—though I don't appreciate the irony—and I don't have a dime to call the sheriff if I want to.

"They took the money."

K whips his long ponytail around.

Leaving the frustration out of his voice, "Maybe the gas station guy will help out. He's been pretty cool. He knows what happened."

If this is true, that makes one of us.

K gives me a bottle of water and a paper towel. I pull the van door closed and make an effort to wash the sweat and goo off my body, reluctant to draw the towel over any skin. The numbness has worn off, the kind protection of shock gone, and even the water stings. Most of me is mashed and abraded and I can't lift my right arm. I make enough progress to give it up and switch into my slip dress, much easier to wear than blue jeans.

I climb into the front seat and look at myself in the van's rear-view mirror. Except for the fingerprint bruises around my neck, I'm startled by how completely the same I look, just dirty and tired. I find my hairbrush and pull it through mats and crusty bits. Eventually, I abandon this effort too. The night is too indelibly stamped on me to be brushed out.

I follow K into the garage, open today. A young mechanic, prematurely grizzled by grease and sun, stares at me as we come in. Despite my dress, I know I stand completely naked, covered in slime, radiating images of the night before. He avoids staring outright, but throws furtive glances my way as K discusses the possibility of van repair.

I stand as still as my inner quaking allows, willing invisibility. I drift with the idea that I should be reacting somehow, but all I can manage is to hold tight. I try listening, but I can't hear anything beyond my own twilight.

Eventually, K takes my hand and leads me back outside. I have no idea how much time has passed. Normal life swirls around, but it has no relevance to me perched here on the edge of nowhere. The golden warmth is gone, but not the distance.

"He'll take a look at the van and fix it for free. He'll help."

So, not everyone here is a pig. This thought gets through, but I keep it to myself.

"Do we need to push it in there?" I am trying to be present.

"Yeah, but you sit down. We'll get it."

The van is soon diagnosed with a cracked head and is beyond repair. Our old friend is gone.

J telephones his parents for help. Sitting on the dusty ground outside the phone booth, K and I listen to his phone call, K's shoulders reddening under the late morning sun.

J's parents agree to fly him home to New York. He hangs up and wrestles with the folding door, momentarily trapping himself inside before it collapses inward, freeing him. K and I stand up, brushing off the dust.

J searches K's face, then stares down at the dirt, his long blond bangs hiding his sky blue eyes."Sorry man. I just can't..."

"It's okay, really. Okay." K sounds sincere enough.

Appearing to be not entirely reassured that he will be forgiven his desertion, J trudges back to the van to gather his things. A bus to Salt Lake stops here, if a prospective passenger waits by the highway. It will take him to the airport.

K can think of no family or friends able to help. My mother and her husband seem our only option. I dread making this call, but if I don't, perhaps even if I do, we will be leaving here on foot.

I step into the phone booth and fold the collapsing door, the enclosed space reassuring. Using a dime borrowed from the young mechanic, I dial the operator and place a collect call.

I cannot imagine telling anyone what happened, let alone my mother and her very correct husband. I plan to say very little, to ask for plane tickets for K and me because of unspecified trouble. My mother answers, accepting the call from the operator.

"Hello? Hello?"

The sound of my mother's voice brushes so gently against the iron rings holding me together that I can't make a sound.

Her voice rises in irritation, "Hello? Hello?"

I struggle to find a voice, afraid she'll hang up before I can speak, afraid I will never have another chance, never find another dime, never have another rational thought.

I squeak out a fraction of a word, "Mom?"

"Dear? Dear, are you all right?"

No, I'm not.

I'm afraid to make a sound. I can't tell this, words have power; speaking threatens to make this real. I struggle for distance so I can keep breathing and standing and living. Sobs choke me, but I know if I start crying, I won't ever stop.

"They…they…Please get me out of here." This is a prayer I shrieked in the night, now I whisper the words into the telephone. The sound of my voice is enough; her one question dies unspoken. If we can get to the airport, tickets for both of us will be waiting.

We have to hurry if we're going to make the bus. We abandon the van, entrusting the keys to the mechanic with a promise to contact him ASAP, and we sift through our few belongings, wrapping the keepers in our sleeping bags. The Yin Yang flag is left behind.

Before leaving this desolate place, I make one more phone call, with another borrowed dime. I can't leave without calling the sheriff.

Folding myself back into the phone booth, I drop the dime in the slot and dial "O," then ask the operator to connect me with the sheriff's office.

I tell the voice that answers that I would like to make a report. I'm referred to someone else. To this voice, I outline the events of the night before and explain that they told me they planned to do this again.

The man on the other end of the line asks no questions, wants no elaboration. He doesn't care where I am, or where I can be reached in California. His disinterest makes clear that he either does not believe me or does not consider this a crime. Whatever protection my rapists have, it extends at least this far.

"Why don't you head home now young lady," he suggests. "Thanks for calling."

By this time, I've grown quite small. I can think of nothing else to say, perhaps ever again, to anyone. The shadow of me still standing here in this phone booth hangs up and pushing open the folding door steps out, blind in the glaring sun.

I travel with K by bus to the airport, I have no idea how we buy bus tickets—perhaps our mechanic benefactor—then onto a plane. We are met at SFO by family I can't fully see, and to whom I can only whisper.

I make it home for my birthday.

Once back at the Atherton house, I am embraced, seemingly forgiven my escapade of the last few months. Even K is made welcome. Here, in anticipation of my expected arrival, a birthday party had been planned. Family has gathered, the festivities haven't been cancelled, kidnapping and rape not yet sinking in here either.

I arrive at the house upright, bedraggled and not-quite-present, but walking about. I am only hours from hanging naked from the ceiling and can still feel the gun barrel pressed against the back of my head, but I am now guest-of-honor for a birthday party.

I have no idea how to behave. Collapse will be rude, hysteria too late. I enter the house wavering between needing to vanish completely and howling at the moon.

No one asks what happened. It isn't mentioned, and I'm less than communicative. *What do I say? To whom do I say it?*

We all slip quickly past why I arrived here as I did. A vague "something bad" floats around but we ignore it. I'm not truly here—I am not entirely anywhere—so I drift among family members, accepting their birthday hugs and going through the motions as they welcome me back, while I struggle to feel as if I actually am.

Mom leads me upstairs, the family dogs follow, and she shows me the room I can use until I "get things back together." She lets me know that I'm to clean up and to come back downstairs for my birthday party. She has left me new clothes to wear.

Once she leaves me, I move slowly. I understand that I'm expected back downstairs and can delay only so long, but I would much rather be alone—much rather.

I close myself in the bathroom and carefully step out of the slip dress, letting it drop to the floor. I can't look at myself in the mirror. I never want to see myself again.

The first few drops of water sting, but I wince through them until the warm shower feels almost good. Finally, with hair washed and in new clothes, I sit on the bedroom floor and consider going back downstairs.

I have no idea how much time passes before I leave the room, but finally I convince myself I have no choice, family is waiting, and since nothing about this can be real, I may as well go along.

I come down the stairs, glancing into the dining room where a table is set with cake and colorful sprinkles, before passing through the doorway into the drawing room. Ahead of me, K, siblings and their friends, and my stepfather and mother sit on fine couches and chairs or stand leaning against the unlit fireplace, all smiling, all waiting for me.

Little Sis perches on the edge of a yellow damask armchair watching expectantly as I descend the stairs. At sight of me, the friend seated beside her—I see now he holds a guitar—strums the familiar opening chords, and my sister's angelic voice lifts to fill the room with the rocker's anthem to those of us on the road. Her sweet voice pierces my heart, and I can't listen beyond "You who are …" before fleeing to somewhere small, dark, and far away.

The family's mumbled concern recedes as I retreat upstairs to my room, then into the closet to hide on the floor, blind and small, the strains of CS&N dwindling to nothing as I escape. I ask those who knock on the bedroom door to let me be alone for a bit and promise I'm just tired. No one sounds convinced but the knocking stops. I hope K offers them an explanation.

I spend the night on the floor, holding myself tight, wondering why I'm not dead. In the morning, I emerge reluctantly, hoping the world has disappeared, but it has not.

My stepfather has arranged for me to have a physical exam. He delivers me to one of his peers, an elderly physician who practices gynecology and psychiatry at Stanford Hospital. For him, I find words to outline the events that brought me to his exam room, if none to explain how I'm feeling about it.

The doctor is a small, grey man, formal and precise. My impression is that what I describe to him is beyond his imagination.

I am polite and cooperative. I restrain myself from assaulting him when he touches me, though all of me wants to smash him flat. He says little, commenting only on my shoulder, strained not dislocated, and notes that my "abrasions will heal." He says nothing of the bruises on my neck; they may be too far north of his particular area of expertise.

He prescribes a strong antibiotic to ward off venereal diseases. As he seems to have avoided mentioning my bruised throat, I don't mention that I couldn't possibly swallow the large pills just yet.

He concludes the appointment by telling me it is important that I "get back on the horse real soon." I assume this is allegorical—there were no horses involved here—and that he means I should be sexually active soon.

This advice seems inappropriate, at best. I choke back the retort that immediately pops to mind, but I'm revolted and dismiss him as well-intentioned but grossly naive. When I get back to my room, I sit in the closet with the door closed and pray again to disappear.

The following day, this physician suffers a serious stroke and dies after unsuccessful surgery. With his passing, I regret my uncharitable opinion of him and entertain the fear that I am now a wrecking-ball in motion—what I described to him was unimaginable, and it took him out.

I hold tight, blind to the outside world. My follow-up appointment is, of course, cancelled.

In addition to finding medical attention for me, my stepfather contacts our local Atherton sheriff, explains the Utah sheriff's dismissal of my attempted report, and sets up an appointment for me to go in to tell him my story. Struggling to be present anywhere, I go when and where directed.

At the sheriff's office, I sit in a metal chair in a room with blackboards and wooden tables. Small windows give glimpses outside of trees and blue sky. Deputies buckled in leather bearing guns, ammunition and billy clubs stand strewn around the room, leaning on the blackboards, hands resting on holsters, shifting their weight from foot to foot. One sits at the table across from me and writes as I talk. The sheriff sits beside him and listens. I'm the only female present.

I grip the chair arms and tell the story from beginning to end, while all of me, except my body, floats around on the ceiling. I tell them of being tricked into accepting the help, of being stripped and hung, of the photos and the rape and rape and rape. I recount snippets of conversation. I describe vehicles, men, equipment.

Listening, the deputies are rapt. The room is hushed except for my voice and the creak of heavy-soled shoes. It smells of aftershave and leather. A humming sets up inside me, and I have trouble responding beyond it. When I finish, one of the deputies states firmly that these men were homosexuals because "no real men would do such a thing." The others mutter agreement.

I add them to my list of the dangerously misinformed.

My body is reenacting Dave's 2001 Space Odyssey final-destination landing sequence, and I can't respond, but I hear them. As the tremors subside, I mutter my appreciation for their time and rise to depart on knees unhappy to bear this burden so soon, but I have to get out. The world is distorted around me, and I can only hope I am polite enough as I bolt from the building.

The Atherton sheriff believes me—my stepfather is respectable and this is a small town. Days later, he invites me to return and to listen in on a call to the Utah sheriff.

The call goes through easily, and the Utah folks are the soul of congeniality. They invite him fishing next time he's in town. But they know nothing about me or the event I have reported, "Sorry we can't be of more help."

My sheriff promises to keep trying. The description of equipment and refusal of local law enforcement to investigate, plus Red's claiming to be a lawyer, suggest to him a need for the FBI.

Within days, my local paper publishes the story with a grab 'em headline about my kidnapping and a desert terror gang. The article states that the Utah attorney general promises a complete investigation. Nothing comes of it, except locally. I manage to smear the night on my mother's new family, too.

No one in the family asks me questions about what happened. We drift past it, and daily life has its own demands. But while my step-siblings and my own Little Sis take school finals, dress for proms, and enjoy swimming parties, I'm struggling to hear and to see. Neither images nor sound will fully resolve. We are indistinct, the world and I.

I struggle to recover something else too, something dramatic that I've lost. I feel its absence, but I'm blind to what it is, or now that it's missing, what it was. I move among family and about the house as a ghost, roaming at night, sleep gone. When alone, I fold myself into the space behind the toilet in the upstairs bathroom and rest as best I can.

Within a few days of arriving, I understand that I have to move on. K has gone already, and I am not expected to stay. I am still "too stressful" for my mother, one stress too many in this new household. Our tensions are old ones and she has not asked details of what happened to me, knowing only the pain in my voice when she agreed to fly me home. We leave it at that. I need to find somewhere else to live.

I know I must, but can find no strength to look for new shelter until I overhear a conversation between my stepfather and mother about my perhaps needing to be hospitalized.

Confined? Under the care of someone who believes they have power over me? Not happening. I vow no one is going to touch me or tell me what to do *ever again*. Anger and fear shake me out of lethargy.

I clamp down. I'm fine, really. No worries here. I stand up. I dress. I smile at the figures around me. I also wrap a Gillette razor blade in tissue and put it in my pocket, just in case, promising myself I'll never again be without a way to escape.

And I find another place to live.

Big Sis allows me to come live in her garage. With her young daughter, she now occupies the home in Palo Alto where we grew up. She works for Ma Bell, and the house is center for friends and their children.

The garage is a garage, not a remodel. My home is a double bed mattress beside the washing machine and hot water heater. I hang a blanket on rope stretched from wall to wall in front, so the garage door can be open without my being on display.

I'm reeling, barely here, barely anywhere. I scurry in and out, hoping no one will see me, leaving only when driven by a physical need I can't ignore. If I stumble through other people, the voices and faces seem kind and concerned. It's unbearable. I want only to hide in my quiet, private space.

A family friend and motorcycle club member lives down the street, and club members are welcome visitors in this house too. Their treasured Harleys frequently sprawl about the driveway, gleaming in the sun. In their colors, the men look menacing, but I know most are family men and many are decorated Vietnam vets.

I'm a few days here when the club president steps into my path as I try to hurry by him and his friends unnoticed. I can't bear to be seen, to be looked at by anyone, even family friends. My heart slams as he brings me to a halt. I stand frozen, staring at the badges on his biker's jacket, frantically trying to disappear rather than let this man see me.

"Can I talk to you for a minute?" His voice is honey. It slices through me, somehow gentleness now more painful than raw cruelty.

I am too involved with forcing myself to remain standing and breathing to follow all of what he says, but by the time he steps away, I understand he has offered to ride to Utah with his friends to put things right. If I want revenge, he offers it. Gallantry does exist; it's clothed in black leather.

I dissolve. He might just as well have stabbed me. Sobbing my appreciation for the offer as I decline it, I retreat to my garage hide-out, hoping as I do that I actually managed to thank him before fleeing.

I wish I could accept. I wish I could say "Yes, I want revenge," but I wouldn't send anyone to that hell, and revenge won't undo what happened. Nothing that I can imagine will remove the slime, the sweat, or the memory, but I love them for their offer, though I'm never able to look directly at any of them, let alone tell them how much I appreciate the gesture.

When the swelling in my throat finally allows me to swallow the pills my deceased physician prescribed, I begin taking them. I dismissed his psychiatric advice, but trust that venereal disease is a real possibility and his medical advice sound enough.

Within a few days of beginning to take them, I am feverish and feel ill, but don't associate it with the antibiotics and continue taking them, until I am too sick to do anything but lie in bed and wait to die. I'm at peace with this inevitability. It's the only option really. I just wish the end would hurry up; I'm very uncomfortable.

The drugs destroy my immune defenses and several misplaced biota take up residence. Soon I can't swallow or breathe or pee. Big Sis checks in after I haven't appeared for a few days and finds me cocooned, waiting for the welcome end.

I'm delivered to the deceased doctor's associate who is bewildered as to why I was taking such massive doses of antibiotics, and I haven't the will to explain it, but he treats me kindly. I endure the exam, too sick to care, and try not to hate him. It will take some weeks, but my body heals.

K departed soon after we got back to California. Now he reappears and wants to go back to Hawaii. I do too. I want to start all over. I want to return to the islands and pretend I never left. I want to purge myself of the last few months.

My family is desperate that I not go. No one thinks this is a good idea except for me. No one is convinced by my assurances that I am fine, really. Big Sis pleads. Mom fusses. Stepfather paces and harrumphs with dignity. I ignore them; I have to try again.

I want Hawaiian sunshine to cleanse me. I want its warmth to heal my ruined self. I want to forget and to disappear in the island's soft embrace. I let my local sheriff know I'm going, just in case they need to reach me. They have no objection, having heard nothing further from Utah. K loans me the fare, and we leave together.

We fly into the familiar Honolulu airport. I've made this trip several times over the last few years. This is beloved territory for me. In the past, I have stepped off the plane and been transported by the warm breeze and the sweet floral perfume drifting from mounds of leis waiting for their visitors.

Not this time. Instead, it's hot and muggy and stinks of jet exhaust. We pass into the terminal, scooping up small paper cups of pineapple juice offered by the vendor, always tangy and cold, but this time cloying and lukewarm.

We leave our few possessions in a locker at the airport and take the bus to Waikiki. Looking for a cheap bed, we wind our way through sweaty crowds on Kalakaua, street traffic noisy and stalled, the still air encasing us in damp fumes. We walk farther and farther away from tourist mecca until finding a place we can afford for a week, all the rent we can muster.

The unit is as cheap a resting place with a real roof and shower as we are likely to find within walking distance of possible job prospects. It's a second floor studio seemingly constructed of bamboo—walls, furniture, lamps.

Footsteps and conversation drift freely through the thin walls. The neighbor next door taps out Morse code long into the night. I find it sinister and suspect him of being a spy.

Once indoors, I find it difficult to leave the confines of this room; everywhere feels dangerous: the neighborhood, the buses, the apartment stairway. I never venture to the beach. The sun isn't warm; it's oppressive. Sunsets don't soothe; they terrify. When I have to go out, I take my darkness with me.

Financial need soon forces me into the street, and I manage to stay outdoors long enough to walk to a restaurant beside the Pink Palace where I apply for a job. Serving food is something I know how to do. I'm hired on the spot. Once safely back at the apartment, I huddle into myself.

I don't show up for my first day of work or any others. I can't force myself to go out in public again so soon.

K is sympathetic, but I have to rally. We need next week's rent. I have to be fine.

While I wrestle with the reality of still being alive and despairing at the loss of the one place that I thought could make everything all right, but find is now paradise hell, the Utah sheriff's office makes contact and asks if I will return to Tooele for a polygraph test.

CHAPTER 6

On the Way It Does

Tooele has relayed their request through the Atherton sheriff. I learn of it when I call home for the sound of voices that don't frighten me.

I place a collect call to the Atherton sheriff. He's apologetic, trying to soften the insinuation that I'm a liar. He heard me tell the story; he believes me.

Hesitating with each word, he explains that the Tooele sheriff wants to make sure the story is true before they go forward. Apparently, his office has caused sufficient ruckus to prod them into action, but given how many weeks have gone by with none, to me, double-checking, my story now seems pointless.

I know they don't believe me, but I don't understand why. I don't understand why they would first imagine me a liar. Why would they expect a young woman to be so evil or deranged? What would I gain from such a lie? Although their ignorance or misinformation is ruining my world just now, in truth, as I consider their request, I'm relieved that I don't know the answers to these questions. I am certain, though, that up to the moment of the collision between my world and theirs, mine has been an infinitely better one.

As incomprehensible to me as their request may be, for whatever reason the Tooele sheriff feels he must protect his community from predatory girls rather than rapists, I have no choice. I haven't enough sense of myself left to raise a reasonable objection or to confront the insult head on, and the Atherton sheriff on the phone is so apologetic, I agree to return to Utah for a polygraph test and hang up the telephone, my supply of righteous indignation exhausted.

Unfolding the payphone door, I slip back upstairs to the safety of my bamboo cage and sit in twilight on the bed, considering the return. I can't imagine it. I don't want to breathe the same air or be lit by the same sun. I don't want to see anyone in Utah, criminals or lawmen, in this case perhaps one and the same, and I particularly don't want them to see me, but I am not about to let them know it. Of course I'll go.

I sit on the bed and pull out of my wallet the neatly-wrapped razor blade I carry with me. Slowly unwrapping it from the tissue, I hold the blade carefully, not wanting to cut my fingers or to bleed on my clothes, and press its thin metal edge against my wrist. It hurts at first. Pushing a little harder, the sharp edge severs the thin skin, and red blood seeps through. I stop then. I don't want to die today. I just need a different hurt, and I need to know I can do it, if I must.

I dab the blood away and carefully re-wrap the razor in new tissue, replacing it in my wallet. It travels with me; no one checks our bags, on or off airplanes.

I return to California alone, leaving K in Waikiki. He's finding the reality here difficult too, and I expect he'll follow me back to the mainland soon. I settle again in my sister's garage.

My stepfather travels to Utah with me. Always formal, in the past we joked that his idea of casual clothes is an old suit, I'm very grateful that he's with me, but I find it impossible to look at him. Rigid with the horror of having to go back, I am more stilted than he.

We are met at the airport by uniformed deputies. They drive us to town in their patrol car and escort us into the sheriff's office. Communications swirl around me and over me and about me but don't include me. My actual physical presence seems to go unnoticed.

I am incidental; my stepfather treated as the only visitor in the room. The message is clear: this is men's business. I have been suspect from the start. Very evidently, my credibility depends upon my male companion.

They chat and mill about. Stepfather sweats profusely in the heat, repeatedly dabbing his glistening forehead with a white linen handkerchief, his customary suit too heavy for hell.

Eventually, I'm introduced to men with uniforms and guns. By now, that's all I see: men and guns. I fight to stay present, to listen and to hear, but I drift away, rattling, increasingly distant. When they speak in my direction, I smile and nod, or hope I have. I need them to like me, to believe me, but I loathe them; I seethe. I don't want to be here. These men could have helped me, should have helped me, and they chose not to. They deserve my fury and my contempt, all my hatred, and all I can do, once again, is to remain silent and wish I could disappear.

With introductions complete, I am asked to sit down in a large wooden chair against the wall and the men return to ignoring me. While I sit, waiting to be wired for their test, I watch officers wrestle a long-haired young man into a room down the hall and listen as they cut off his long hair while he pleads with them to stop. The sounds grow stifled and the door is finally slammed shut.

I struggle to hold still, fighting not to fight, hatred consuming me. I'm overwhelmed with certainty that everyone here should die and that great pain and humiliation should be involved. I rock in my wooden chair grasping the armrests, frightened into complete silence, desperately wishing I could be gone, wishing again that Thug had just pulled the damn trigger. I lose my battle to stay present, blessedly.

I hold onto the chair and drift to the far-away place, above and beyond, and from the safety of my gold cocoon watch the men mill about below. The golden man isn't with me, but the warmth and distance are.

Eventually, someone decides a polygraph is unnecessary. A voice informs me. I can't see faces. In the room below, shoulders relax, shuffling ceases. The men seem relieved.

My stepfather's deteriorating appearance may decide it. He is sweating profusely, mopping his soaked forehead with the damp handkerchief clearly no longer up to the task. I wish it were because they find me credible, but since I have been asked nothing and have barely spoken a word, I can only assume they decide it's not worth their time, or fear a heart attack is imminent, a fear that is not, in fact, out of the question.

I am unable to summon relief or gratitude. It's too late for that. I am lost and on automatic pilot. They ask if I'm willing to drive out to look at a suspect. Little is registering.

Sure, let's go.

We drive to a construction site in the midst of nowhere, and a tall man with stringy black hair sets down his tools and approaches the car. It could almost be Lanks, but I don't think it is. I am only slightly present, and I can't get much of a look, everything indistinct and far away, but I say "No." The officers are unreadable. They drive us back to the airport in silence. I may have let one of the rapists go.

Stepfather and I fly back to SFO sweat-soaked and exhausted. I am shamed to silence for exposing him to this. We part without discussion of the day, and I go home to the Palo Alto garage, folding myself into the safety of my small, dark space.

Although each dawn arrives with a dose of paralyzing dread, the sun keeps rising, and my heart goes on beating. I wake on my mattress in the garage with both tears and the relevant song lyrics poised.

Why the hell does the sun go on shining?

It just can't be right.

I am pulled to stay in darkness, the razor blade kept close, and although I need to know instant death is within my grasp, I really don't want to die disgracefully. I don't want to hurt my family's feelings. When I need reassurance, I press the blade's edge hard enough against my wrist for the thin red line to appear, but I won't slice through this flesh just yet because if I do, the rapists win, and that wouldn't be right either.

So, despite having no will to do it, I go through the motions of being alive: I wake up, I walk about, I get hungry and thus, before long, I have to find a way to earn a living. I have to be fine.

I have now what feels to me like an internal hum that makes interaction with other people difficult or impossible. If someone else is in it, it's hard for me not to rattle myself out of the room. When the hum intensifies, both sight and sound distort, leaving my response to the unfortunate soul who is attempting to communicate with me, questionable. Under this limitation, job-hunting looms as an insurmountable obstacle.

Big Sis rescues me once more. She works for Ma Bell and arranges an interview for me at headquarters in downtown Palo Alto. I arrive on time for the appointment at the formidable old brick building. Nervous, once seated for the interview, I have to pat the chair to make sure I remain sitting in it.

The interview goes well enough. The lady speaking to me from across the table has deep brown hair and smells of gardenia. She passes me along for testing.

I pass the tests, however I'm turned down for the job as a telephone operator because I have done too well.

"You'll be bored," Ms. Gardenia notes, flashing a conspiratorial smile.

I can't accept the decision, another interview being out of the question, my nerves shot. I plead. I pledge loyalty. I allude to childhood dreams of serving as a long-distance operator.

As I work up to tears, I dump my desperation on her, if not the truth. I am not in dire need of the position; this is my first interview. Beyond this, I haven't yet looked for work, but I cannot bear the idea of doing so, human contact and scrutiny too excruciating.

The idea of additional interviews curdles my stomach. I have nothing to say about myself and I hate to be looked at. As far as I'm concerned, I am still smeared with scum, standing naked in public no matter what clothing I actually wear. Looking closely, anyone can see that most of me still lies huddled on the underground room floor. I cannot bear the idea of more scrutiny.

I beg.

Because Big Sis is a legend in this office, remembered as a superstar who has moved on to higher things, I succeed in convincing Ms. Gardenia that the talent runs in the family, and that I, too, will be a superior long-distance operator. Overriding her own better judgment, she gives me the job.

She was correct, I am soon bored and hate the work, but remain at the position for a year before exploding.

Wearing headsets, operators sit on high stools in a cavernous room facing walls of plugs, holes, cords, and lights. A light comes on. The operator grabs a cord, plugs it in, "Operator."

A voice makes a request, usually for help with a call or an emergency. I panic and plug my first screaming caller into the fire department before actually hearing what he wants. I trust it turned out okay—firemen can do almost anything and have all the other emergency numbers. I repeat this to myself several times hoping it's true.

Occasionally, an older voice asks for "Central," a holdover from an earlier time. Others ask for the time of day, weather reports, or recipe advice.

Some days I'm a good operator, but most days I'm not. Usually, the callers infuriate me. I find them stupid and rude, and those who call from loneliness to speak with the anonymous, ubiquitous "Operator" break my heart.

I keep up appearances. I go to work and go back to the garage before breaking down. I can't sleep. I'm always sick to my stomach. I fall to pieces at any hint of kindness or sentimentality. I can't bear to face the mornings and want only to hide in the dark. But I don't die.

Men approaching me anywhere, the hall, the street, the grocery aisle, cause a flush of adrenaline panic that leaves me sick and exhausted. I am forever crossing aisles, changing directions, leaving rooms.

I used to love to dance, to enjoy music of all kinds. Now, I can't bear the joy in it. The soundtrack to my teenage life is especially off limits, the ache it triggers so enormous that it threatens to engulf me and never let me out. My music is from the before-times, and I can't visit there anymore.

I still believe in a centered being. I believe I might touch the Eternal if I could just calm down. The idea was set early in my life—it was all the rage—and hasn't left me, and the despair I'm beginning to feel has something to do with this, with the loss of any hope I might have of ever again being in the Light.

As the days go on, I grow increasingly ashamed. I don't understand the hole I've fallen into. I know I've lost something important, but I don't know what it is. And in spite of how wrong it seems, the cruel night can't have been as dreadful or significant as it seems to me; the world didn't come to an end, and everyone else seems to have moved on.

I try hard to talk myself out of the despair. The men embarrassed me. I was humiliated. So what? I got off lucky, as they said repeatedly. I'm not physically maimed. No permanent damage is evident. But still, I wish they had shot me, rather than leave me in this dark place.

I know I must be doing something wrong, or that there is just something wrong with me, but I can't figure out what it is or what to do about it. I try another psychiatrist.

This doctor's office occupies a corner in the new Stanford Medical Center. The office is large and well-appointed in mahogany and leather. Bookcases full of serious medical tomes line the walls.

I settle on the edge of an armchair.

The physician himself is middle-aged and also very well-appointed, his hair dark and carefully combed, his hands manicured and smooth, his suit tailored, and his tie fine.

He begins, "So, my dear, what brings you here?"

He sits behind an enormous desk. Its gleaming surface stretches yards between us. I sit across from him, both hands holding onto the armchair, and begin the story. I chant it this time, scrolling through the set-up, the rapes, the gun, and the official dismissal. I keep my eyes on the desktop and my internal vibration roars in my ears. I tell him I'm afraid all the time and that I can't sleep, I can't bear to be looked at or touched, and that I'm worried. I hold the armrests and keep going until I'm through it.

He listens, brow furrowed, lips pursed, staring at me across the spacious desk, his forearms resting on its gleaming surface, hands clasped together, white cuffs exposing tan wrists.

When I finish, he is silent. He sits immobile long enough to unnerve me further. Finally, settling into his grand, leather swivel chair, leaning it back a bit, in a solemn tone he asks, "Isn't it about time you got over it?"

His perfunctory remark is brutal, hitting me in the pit of my stomach like a punched fist. I agree with the gist of it, but need something more right now, perhaps if only less abrupt, and although what I need remains unclear to me, it's immediately apparent that despite the furnishings and grooming, this man hasn't a clue either.

I leave shocked, feeling worse than when I came in. He manages to insult me and to confirm my worst fears simultaneously: I am flawed for not gracefully handling gang rape and it is my responsibility to work that out.

As the doctor so helpfully stated, I need to "get over it." Insecurity radiates off me. I vibrate and flutter. I am not a reassuring presence. Attempts at internal healing having failed, I take a stab at improving my appearance, a tangible effort to fix what's wrong with me. I enroll in modeling school, hoping classes will leave me polished enough to be comfortable in public, if not truly relaxed. I need to disguise the fact that I am actually walking around naked covered in slime.

I can think only of how to fix this part of my ruined self. Whatever else is wrong remains a mystery.

This will be my second round of modeling classes, first trying them at age fifteen. This time, I enroll at Barbizon Modeling School, planning to learn how to feign self-confidence. I had little enough before the kidnapping, but now I'm not even sure I am still alive, let alone a competent human being, so I'm not looking for real confidence, just tools to paint the face of it.

Saturdays, I attend classes in San Francisco and regain my pivot. I learn to wear false eyelashes and to sculpt eyes and cheekbones with a rainbow of colored powders. I survive a photographic session, working hard to keep pain from memory of the pornographic Polaroids out of sight. The fashion photographer never knows how afraid I am of throwing-up on him.

The photos are good. I am unrecognizable.

A few weeks in, I dress in my suede mini-skirt, hooded orange sweater, and full makeup for class in the city. My mother loans me her Austin Healey for the drive on this particular day. Class goes well. I can pivot in any direction.

Leaving class, I walk quickly back to the parking garage, fighting the urge to run, making an effort to apply in public what I've learned in class: head high, shoulders relaxed and no vomiting on the sidewalk.

Finally reaching the car, what passes for safety to me here, I settle myself into the Healey's low seat. The sleek sports car is meant for longer legs than mine. I wriggle down a little to reach the pedals, the position leaving me low-riding. I try to embrace the image.

Late afternoon sun glints off the bay. A gusting breeze chases leaves and litter up the street. I leave the top of the Healey up although it's almost warm enough to put it down, but the canvas takes some babying to cradle into its nest, and I'm not dressed for the effort.

The car's engine roars to life and I maneuver out onto Market Street. As I pull into traffic, a limousine pulls up beside me and a front seat passenger rolls down the window. I can see into the imposing vehicle a bit. There seem to be several men wearing gold jackets inside. I assume drug dealers or a band.

As I try to find my place in traffic, a mustachioed, gold-jacketed man leans out the limo window and whirls his arm around, apparently encouraging me to roll down my window too.

I do. He seems frantic.

"Hey, wanna go see Tom Jones?" He hollers out the window.

I flash several thoughts before speaking. I don't laugh out loud, though I may have smiled, not trying too hard to hide my amusement at such a ridiculous question.

No, I don't want to see *Tom Jones*. My *grandmothe*r listens to him. He must be fifty years old! I am practically a Dead Head, after all.

But I do remember seeing his name on the Circle Star billboard as I drove past this morning. From the question, I decide the men in the limo aren't drug dealers, they may be his band.

Traffic crawls along. We inch forward, our cars remaining side-by-side. I shift back to neutral and rev the engine to keep it running. The mustachioed gentleman in the gold jacket hangs out his window, smiling, waiting for my answer.

I ponder saying yes. This is a chance to be spontaneous, maybe have fun. Except for the vague terror that rides my shoulders, I have no reason to say no.

I rev the engine again and watch him smiling. The rock-and-roller still lurking in my heart says "Do it." Music is good and great. Head high, shoulders back, give it a go.

"Sure," I call back out the car window, hoping he can hear me over the Healey's roar.

He slaps the car side and grins, "Pull in behind us and stay close."

When the limo pulls forward, I cut in behind. It takes the first right. I follow and the limo turns again.

I have made this drive many times, back and forth on Bayshore. I know how to get to the highway, and this limo is doing it all wrong. I follow, but my heart starts pounding. I'm afraid I've made another mistake.

We've turned into a narrow back street heading into the labyrinth south of Market. Panic takes over. I must have been mistaken again: they are druggies, not musicians. I'm going to be trapped. They're going to stop and block me in. I'm in trouble.

My whole body starts shaking. The trembling makes it hard to hold the steering wheel, and my foot won't stay steady on the pedals, jerking about, racing and lugging the engine in turns. I struggle not to stall the powerful engine, desperate that it keeps running so I can make my escape when pressed.

Whipping my head back and forth, I search for a side street to dart into, but we pass only alleyways even more narrow, where I would surely be trapped.

The limo in front of me keeps moving.

Suddenly, a freeway entrance opens in front of us, and without pause we are heading south on Hwy. 101 having bypassed downtown traffic. It's an entrance I've never seen. They are not luring me to fates unknown; they're taking a shortcut.

It takes me a few miles to calm, to accept that I'm not to be dragged from my car by crazed drug dealers. I shake the cramps from my hands and rethink what I'm doing.

I reassure myself. I am just heading home after a day of classes. I'm invited to a show in a town from which I could walk home. Why not? I want this to be Fun. Fear is exhausting. I breathe hard and decide to live through it.

Sure, let's go see Tom Jones.

We approach San Carlos and the limo takes the exit. I follow. As we slow to enter a permit-only gate behind the theater, the limo driver gestures in my direction and a guard then waves both vehicles through. We drive into a large parking lot, and I lose track of the limo as I look for my own parking.

I pull the Healey into a safe enough spot, no car doors too near on either side, and step out. As I slam the door closed, my arm is swept up by the mustachioed gentleman. He tucks me close and tells me, "Tom can't wait to meet you."

We walk arm-in-arm through the back entrance of the theater. I'm too startled to do anything but hope my eyelashes are still on straight. As we go in, Mr. Mustache explains that he is Tom's manager and that Tom was in the limo and loves the Healey.

At the revelation, I am very grateful I didn't laugh out loud at the initial invitation as it was called out the car window; some rudeness cannot be undone.

We navigate a short hall and turn to face a door, open slightly, with a large star emblazoned on it. A small crowd fills the room inside. We push through the others and my escort leads me to the far corner of the room where Mr. Jones sits on a white couch, grinning, as he watches me approach.

CHAPTER 7

Flaunting a Lady

Tom is gracious, raving about the beautiful car I drive and wanting to know all about it. He asks my name, introducing me to people he seems to expect I'll recognize, but don't. The room is jammed when I first enter. I notice now that the crowd is thinning; others are taking their leave. Within minutes of my entrance, the last to be in the room with us, Mr. Mustache, smiles, says goodbye and closes the door, leaving us alone in the small room.

Tom sits casually on the sofa that lines one wall, his arms extended to either side, resting easily along the sofa back. I stand frozen a few feet away. He pats the back of the couch.

Despite my earlier dismissal, I see now that my grandmother had more sense than I knew: he is gorgeous. Although I am too rattled to fully appreciate it, I am not dead.

Hysteria can take only so many forms. Realizing the apparent gross misunderstanding, and reconsidering my worry about the whole band, I start to laugh, between giggles choking out the situation from my perspective.

"Do they bring you girls before every show? Is this pre-game warm-up?" I dab at my eyes, hoping not to laugh the eyelashes off.

He laughs too and deflects my questions, asking about me. I tell him the truth about the Austin Healey. I know he thinks I'm somebody—the makeup and the car make an impression—but I confess I'm a telephone operator and that the car is my mother's.

He brushes aside the disclosures, seemingly unfazed, but tells me I have to leave; he has to dress for the show. Whatever warming up was to be, he's out of time.

As if on cue, a team pours in to help him dress. Mr. Mustache leads me back out into the hallway, to a spot behind the scenes where I can stand to watch the show.

I wait with various hangers-on as roadies and musicians bustle about, getting it right. We quiet once the show begins, small groups clustered at thruways to listen and watch.

The warm-up act, a comedian, gets some raunchy laughs before Tom makes his entrance. To adoring applause, surrounded by handlers, Tom is escorted to the stage dressed now in a skintight outfight that I wasn't allowed to watch him wriggle into.

Adoring women fill the audience. Many have used a heavy hand with eyeliner and rat-tail combs. They are an enthusiastic bunch, pleading out their love for him, repeating his name tinged with ecstasy. Some dash to the stage and in desperation hurl their underwear at him.

He keeps singing.

At the end of the set, the backstage hall floods again with musicians, crew, and purpose. The stage empties past me with much hushed exclamation and meaningful, if unintelligible, gesturing among them. The show went well, I assume.

I back against a wall and hope no one notices that I'm a true malingerer. Abruptly, while the stage is still clearing, Mr. Mustache reappears, and whirling my arm once again under his own, maneuvers me to a stairway which we ascend. As we climb, he pats my arm and tells me Tom really enjoys my company and that I am joining him for dinner.

"Do you like Chinese?"

I'm wound tight. I have my model façade on: shoulders back, chin up. I keep my physical reaction under control. My knees shake but don't give out. Stomach cramps will prevent my actually eating anything, but I will be civilized about it.

Why does it have to be Chinese?

"Yes, of course." I put a smile behind it.

We reach the top of the stairs and emerge through the doorway into a large lounge. Several people hang about. Tom rests on a sofa. I am escorted to him and presented once more.

I'm trying to have fun, while being paralyzed and needing to vomit. I sit down and feign my own presence. We chat. I must respond—he keeps chatting.

Soon enough, Chinese food arrives, this time on faux-silver platters and served by young men in white jackets. The scent of ginger fills the room. I hold a plate of won ton and pretend to be too fascinated by the goings on around me—star struck—to eat.

I am actually fighting the need to knock Tom's hand off my neck, where it now rests as he casually fiddles with my hair and chats with his entourage. That first moment of flesh on flesh sears into me, and then settles to a sad burn, the difference between gentle affection and brutality, a distinction I am unable to make.

Tom sports an imposing ring on one finger and catches me looking at it.

"From Sammy Davis," he tells me as he admires it himself. He sets his hand back on my shoulder, lies his head back against the couch and promptly falls asleep. He must be running on fumes. I've never seen anyone fall asleep so quickly.

Secured under his forearm as it rests across my shoulders, I hold as still as I can manage and let him sleep. Everyone else hushes too. They eat, drift about and whisper. Finally, Mr. Mustache touches Tom's arm to wake him—show time.

The hall and dressing room bustle again as performers prepare for their second show. I loiter just outside the open dressing room door, one of the gang now, and try to stay out of the way. A petite woman touches my arm and asks if I think it would be all right if she went inside to meet Him. I'm staring at Lassie's human mother. She couldn't be more real, and exactly what I might expect without Lassie actually present.

Delighted by the encounter, I am the gracious hostess, "Of course, please come in."

I lead her through the door and up to Tom. "May I introduce…"

Thank goodness he doesn't need the name because all I can remember is "Lassie's mother." She finishes the sentence, stepping warmly into his personal space and extending her hand, "June, please."

I withdraw and let her fantasize.

As the second show begins, I am invited to wait in an adjoining room. Mr. Mustache tells me a party is planned after the show, and Tom hopes I'll join them.

"After that, we hope you'll come with us to Las Vegas." He leaves the thought dangling as he heads out of the room.

It seems unlikely to me that I will do either of these things, but I try to enjoy this as a flattering, if presumptuous invitation, and not as an insulting and life-threatening one. My perspective is ruined.

I sit alone in this room for a very few minutes. It soon fills with what appears to be a harvest of buxom, big-haired women from the audience. They understand that they have been invited to an after-show party.

Two or three men seem to be doing the gathering, including the evening's host, a local radio DJ. At one point, he cruises past me, slowing and taking a good look.

Mr. Mustache shoos him away, muttering as he does so, "No, she has Tom's brand on her."

I am in over my head.

I retreat to the dressing room to hide, aware I'm not prepared for so much adventure, but still considering hanging-in for the after-party.

Unfortunately, I am not alone in the dressing room. The opening act comedian is hiding here too. I head to the opposite couch and begin to sit down.

"No, no. Don't sit," he whines. "Wanna watch those legs."

He continues while I hang half-seated, "What color underwear you wearing?"

Is this relevant?

I straighten.

He whines once more, "Why you waiting for Tom? I make the same dough he does."

A donkey bray escapes him.

That's it—fun just isn't what it used to be. My façade crumbles. I call him an asshole and storm out, back to the parking lot and the Healey, a safe place. He keeps up the bray as I flee.

I drive home shaking, furious with myself for everything: for going to the show in the first place; for not being cool enough to be a slut; for not asking the jerk what color underwear he was wearing; and for not telling Mr. Jones my ditching him wasn't personal.

Soon after my failure as a groupie, K too abandons his dream of a good life in Hawaii and he reappears. His is the only human presence I can fully tolerate. Although I begrudge the complete failure of chivalry, I don't hate him or fear him. He assures me he and J weren't in on it. I have no one else to believe.

I move out of my sister's garage, and he and I rent an apartment in old Palo Alto. The unit reminds me a little of Waikiki, the small cottages that in earlier times strung behind the Market Place with flowering bushes lining the walkways. We settle into an end unit facing its twin across a modest lawn.

Our facing neighbor is an air-traffic controller at SFO. She shrieks at us across her courtyard if she hears us speaking; our voices infuriate her. She wanders about muttering that she needs her rest. We agree, and take to whispering when we're home.

I dislike the job as a telephone operator as much as Ms. Gardenia predicted. I hate sitting in one place for so many hours. I am bored by the repetitive work. I dislike my co-workers, and the customers make me furious.

I'm angry all the time. Trying to make a meal, I let an egg slip through my fingers and it smashes on the floor. I pull the next egg from the carton too roughly and it breaks in my hand. Furious at the waste I cannot afford, I grab the whole carton and hurl it at the wall, then hide in the bathroom for an eternity, toying with the razor, slashing thin red lines across my wrists.

In despair over the constant, lurking rage, ashamed at myself for everything I have ever done, I wedge myself behind the toilet, the only place I can find to hide, and hope I never have to face anyone, especially myself, ever again. I don't know what's wrong, but I'm certain I can't go on living if it's going to feel this way.

When I finally emerge, K has made the dinner.

Other than him, I'm suspicious of everyone, even myself. I doubt my instincts, my ability to accurately judge a situation. I have no reliable measure left to decide who might be a friend and who might be a mortal enemy. I waved off the first two men, but the second two fooled me, and if I can be fooled so easily, then most particularly, I can't be trusted.

K finds work at the pool hall on California Avenue and we leave the angry flight controller behind, moving nearby to the back unit in a duplex on Alma. The front unit is occupied by a weightlifter friend of

K's and his tiny girlfriend. She speaks to me through her screened mail slot sometimes as I pass by their door.

As winter closes in, though it's only mildly windy and wet, riding my bike to work wears me down. I love the ride through old Palo Alto, the quiet wooded streets a haven for the few minutes I pass through, but with the colder weather, I need a car.

Having saved five-hundred dollars, I walk up Page Mill Road to the trailer park across El Camino Real and buy a grey, '64 VW Beetle from a newlywed couple selling the older of their two Bugs. Its license, BMP 209, it quickly becomes Bump and is my ride for the next 16 years.

Work becomes a bit easier with the commute cut to a few minutes, and I slip into the shadow of work and restless hours off as a substitute for life.

I've lost perspective on everything. I weigh each activity against its downside: I might end up hanging naked from the ceiling. Not much overcomes the burden. I go to work and come home quickly, very little else draws me out.

But in a moment of saving grace, I am lured out of my bleak routine by an invitation that meets the high threshold: one I cannot refuse. A co-worker's dog has had puppies, nine black lab/golden retriever pups. They're ready for homes. I lie to myself and agree to "just go look."

Soon after, I drive BMP down El Camino Real to their home in Sunnyvale. My co-worker opens the door to a room awash in fluffy, wiggly piles of life. They bound and scrabble and tumble over one another, practicing growls and high-pitched yips.

I kneel down into the midst of the swirling, black furry piles, struggling not to cry. Their soft fur, their sweet smell, hurts. I haven't tolerated, let alone welcomed, the touch of any other living thing for many months. From this isolation, I am saved by the warm, shaggy bundle that climbs onto my lap and makes me his.

My new puppy quickly becomes my very best friend and beloved companion. His touch doesn't make my skin crawl or my stomach roil.

He binds me to the earth, my savior. He will be my raison d'être for many years. I name him Beaujangles, and together we drive back to Palo Alto in BMP.

While I'm working and holding on to my new puppy for life, the Atherton sheriff, as he suggested he would do in our second meeting, has contacted the FBI. He suspects a law-enforcement cover-up, if not outright involvement in the kidnapping. As could be expected, the FBI began their investigation by contacting the person whose name K used when he first called the Tooele sheriff to report my kidnapping—understandable, but unfortunate. This leads them to K's true identity and to the fact that he is wanted for draft evasion.

I leave work one afternoon and a long black sedan with tinted windows idles in the No Parking zone out front. Two Suits in sunglasses get out quickly, present their badges in unison, and the older asks if they might speak to me. They are FBI, and they claim the part.

They want me to sit in the car to look through a book of suspects' photographs. Opening the car door, they invite me to get in the back seat. I cover the short distance to the car before I find an excuse to decline or a hole large enough to swallow me. I slide into the back seat and take the large photo album onto my lap. The older Suit speaks, but I'm too frightened to actually listen. Neither seems to notice.

The older finishes his explanation and goes silent. It must be time for me to look. I open the album to its first page. Both Suits sit in the front seat with sunglasses still on, turned to watch me flip the pages.

I turn each unwieldy page slowly and scan photographs of hundreds of men in various stages of dissolution, sickeningly afraid I might recognize a face while hoping desperately that I will. Finally, without success, I turn the final page and close the book. None of these criminals are mine.

With the cover story for their interview concluded, the Suits turn to the real reason they are here. Do I know where K is? In somber tones they ask if I understand that concealing a draft dodger is a federal offense.

Do I understand they can send me to prison for not cooperating? Do I understand I am a criminal for concealing him?

I assure them I don't know where he is—I don't know precisely, that is true—and that I understand that I, too, may be a criminal.

We repeat this charade a few days later with another book of photos and another denial, only this time they assure me I should cooperate. The older one slides his glasses down his nose and lets me see his eyes as he outlines the precariousness of my position. His eyes tell me no more than the sunglass lenses. I see an enemy.

The following morning the Suits march up the walkway to our apartment, and K jumps out the bathroom window with a toothbrush in his mouth, leaping the back fence into our neighbor's yard and disappearing. I answer the door and deny again knowing where he is. If they want my help, they'll have to be more specific.

I stand and face them, waiting to be arrested. My heart slams.

I can't do this, I can't be arrested.

I wobble at the edge. This can't happen, spiraling: *I can't leave Beau, I'll lose my job, I'm not properly dressed, I have no shoes to wear...* I pull myself back to the doorstep where I'm standing facing the two Suits.

I'm not going to prison. This is not right.

The men wear their mirrored sunglasses, as always. I think it's the same elder, but that the younger of the two is new. I can't read personal truth through the lens' darkness but I scramble, betting conscience does lurk behind them.

"Have you found my kidnappers?"

The younger agent hardly flinches, but I see he twitches a bit in the direction of the other, the one who did watch me look through the books and knows exactly what I mean.

"We are looking for Mr. K."

"Yes, I know, but you started out looking into why the Utah sheriff won't investigate my kidnapping, and I haven't heard anything."

I'm certain the silence doesn't last as long as it feels.

"Are you able to tell us where Mr. K is?"

"No."

The older Suit chews on it. The next move is his. Young Suit now has his face turned fully towards the other. I presume he's staring too.

The Vietnam War is a horrible mistake that most Americans see as such. We are in the streets in protest; we've been there for a few years. Veterans bringing their broken selves home are a public embarrass-ment. Unfortunately, as always, legislation is several steps behind. Law enforcement is applying rules few support, and which under scrutiny constitute rather reprehensible moral violations. Arresting the friend of a draft dodger may constitute one of these.

He must be weighing this. I'm hopeful, and apparently, to his credit, he decides that adding insult to injury, even for God and Country, will not be necessary today. I am not going to jail.

Old Suit holds out a card, "Call if you have any information for us."

I take it from his extended hand and let out an overdue breath.

The Suits turn in unison and walk away. Young Suit tilts his head slightly toward the other as their backs recede. He appears to be listening intently to old Suit. I watch them depart, head to head, and imagine the elder's deadpan voice describing the lurid circumstances that brought them to my doorstep. I wonder how explicit he will be. I hope he leaves it vague, but I'm not hopeful.

I don't hear from them again about draft evasion or my own kid-napping, although another two Suits do appear two years later to arrest me for involvement in the Patty Hearst kidnapping.

I am alleged to have driven the getaway car, a VW Bug. A former neighbor, whose religion is offended by my mother's marital history, holds out hope that our family might be responsible for something pun-ishable and fingers me for the crime. And, although the car is the wrong color and I the wrong ethnicity, for her I fit the profile closely enough.

These Suits look for me first in Atherton. My mother claims to not know where I am, lying bald-faced to the Suits. *Go Mom.*

She does know exactly where I am, and her reaction to their visit makes me wonder if she was a bit afraid I might be involved. Big Sis has no such reservations and easily gives me up. Once onto me, it doesn't take much for them to rule me out.

But here in Palo Alto, watching these Suits retreat, will be the last I see of the FBI myself, I hear nothing further from them about the kidnapping.

K returns in a few days and we resume our shadow lives.

Some weeks later, a sheriff's deputy reaches me at work on the break-room phone, to tell me two men in Tooele have been arrested for a crime similar to what I described, and they are going to trial. This time the girl is a local runaway, thirteen-years-old.

I shrink as I listen to him. My demeanor annoys a co-worker who sneers as she flicks her cigarette ash off on the rug behind her, "Oh, please, it couldn't be that bad."

I hear her remark as I spin around on the ceiling. I fight the urge to beat the smoker to death for her stupidity but don't, though I long regret deciding against it.

This is my fault. I let this happen. I am a coward. I should have worked harder to find them. I deserve to die.

I want to. I wish I didn't want to go on living just a little longer, even though I'm filled with loathing every morning as it dawns. I am sorry beyond words that I let this happen to another girl, a little girl. There is no pit deep enough.

The deputy says I may be called for a statement and to stay within reach. I do, but I'm not contacted. He calls again not long after, the last I hear from law enforcement for many years, to let me know the two accused men were acquitted. The evidence disappeared. And he doesn't say, but I understand, the girl was a young runaway with no credibility, easily labeled another liar.

Despite my new puppy, at work my attitude deteriorates to a point of administrative concern. Operators are not known for their cordiality, but Ma Bell aspires to a certain civility and doesn't condone the openly surly or snide. I frequently cross the line.

Ms. Gardenia takes me into the back room for a conference. We sit at a large table, corner and end. She reminds me how great an employee my sister had been. Why can't I be more like her? They have high hopes for me too. I can fill her shoes. They know I have it in me.

She finishes, after expressing her understanding that I'm young and she knows a job interferes with playtime and that "sometimes we just have to do things we don't want to do."

The extreme truth of her observation breaks a barrier I work hard to hold onto in public. I bite the scream that rises, fighting to keep from screeching my awareness of this truth and my vehement objection to it into her gentle face. I want to shriek at her that this is a truth that will no longer apply to me. No acquiescence, ever again. Hyperbole be damned.

Her innocence and well-meant advice to the foolish young woman she sees seated before her, the girl who refuses to accept her role, her position, her fate, makes me so furious I want to kill her and myself at the same time.

I cling to the chair and waver between my two options: beat her up or do absolutely nothing. Nothing is my best option, once again.

Swallowing the fury leaves me speechless. I sit still and explode inside. The anger whirls my real self around the room as it gushes from me.

At the table, I smile and squeak out a promise to try. When I can breathe and move again, I leave the room and spend the remainder of my work-shift shaking it off in the ladies' room. I'm dinged for the missed time.

CHAPTER 8

Sweet Jane M.I.A.

By the time I quit, the things I hate about being a telephone operator are many, but this is the beginning of my year-after-year change in employment, a change that always seems necessary to me at the time. In each instance I find justification, a good enough reason, to walk away from the job.

Most likely, working as a telephone operator is not as dreadful as I find it to be, but my time is up. Unable to bear the work or contact with the other employees any longer, I give a proper two-weeks' notice as is expected of respectable employees. The reason I give: I'm going back to college and will need more flexible hours. This is what I write down, though I have no actual plan. School is a dream, and the need for flexibility, an outright lie.

The day I give notice, I'm scheduled to work through the night on graveyard shift. I complete the termination paperwork and hand it to the night supervisor who shakes her head but makes no comment. Clearly, I'm a disappointment.

I take a seat and put on my headset. The night drags on. We are few at the board and the supervisor has set an alarm to ring whenever a call comes in so we can fade off between them.

Many nights are very slow; some operators find the bell useful. I, however, don't sleep anyway, and I'm sitting right underneath the bell. Every time it rings, I'm startled and annoyed, increasingly so as we approach the wee hours. I'm watching the board and feel a bit insulted that the supervisor assumes I need to be roused to do my job. I'm touchy.

The bell goes off one time too many for my limited patience. I stand up and flip it off.

As I sit down, Madam Supervisor stalks over, her high heels clicking across the linoleum squares. I pointedly ignore her and keep my eyes on the board. She pauses only a moment before telling me to leave the board and to come with her.

I follow her into the room of my last meltdown. She closes the door and turns to address me. "Why did you turn that off?" She asks in an I-don't-give-a-shit-what-your-explanation-is-but-I-have-to-ask tone.

"It's annoying. I can't stand it."

"It is to stay on."

"We don't need it on."

"I decide that. Don't touch it again."

And of course I must respond, having already given my notice. *How can I not?* "What are you going to do? Fire me?"

She has me escorted from the building. I was leaving anyway, but now I forfeit my final two-week paycheck.

I have lasted a year.

I have no leeway, no resources to fall back on, surviving paycheck to paycheck, and family, who in other times might have helped had I been able to bring myself to ask, have their own lives, difficulties, and pain. My world, my problem. A dreaded job hunt looms again.

I weigh my options: get another job or die. Death is the more appealing of the two, but now I have Beau. He nestles on my lap, soft and warm, gentle and innocent. He needs me. I owe him life. So, I have to leave the safety of my bedroom and go find another way to earn a living. Beau and I need to eat.

A return to waitressing seems the least horrible option. I know the work, the feel of the floor and my place on it. The interviews should be tolerable. Despite the dread in my belly and the constant hum of worry that nags at me, I'm confident that at the very least, I can feign pleasant serving-wench through a daily work-shift.

Big Boy Restaurants has a franchise in Mountain View. The layout, procedures, and menu are nearly identical to the store in Denver—bless franchises. I can do this. I present well: dressed up, experienced. I don't have to jump through any hoops. The balding manager hires me on the spot.

I was the "best waitress they ever had" in Denver, or so the manager told me, but that waitress has vanished. Right off the bat, I can't work the counter, my first station, because I can't make eye contact with the customers, and I hate them for looking at me. I quickly lose track of whose order goes where, and whether I face a new customer waiting to order, or one whose dishes I have cleared and who is waiting for a check. I forget everything, except that I'm on display behind this counter.

In Denver the sad old men, in reality just worn, perhaps not so old, who hung around at the counter sipping cups of lukewarm coffee, eyeing the waitresses as we worked, used to stir my pity. They watched us in our short skirts, salivating in hopes of snatching an especially juicy glimpse of thigh or buttock when we reach to grab condiments or lean over to drop dirty dishes into bins. Their need and loneliness seemed comprehensible, even familiar, sometimes.

But here, now, they are scum whose worthless souls stain the universe. Their eyes on me burn my flesh. The very idea that they can see me keeps my stomach churning. When one of the lurkers makes a mildly lewd comment, I have to be restrained by the restaurant manager, who prevents me from leaping over the counter and beating the sorry puke who spoke to me to a bloody mass. The manager, confused by my instant fury, leads me outside to cool off instead.

I'm not assigned to the counter again. I do better at table service where I needn't look directly at the customers. I can focus on the tabletop and need remember only which sides of the table are occupied, not what customers look like or who they are. And I'm not trapped, as I am behind the counter. On the floor, I can move away from stares, and when I can't stand it any longer, when I must escape, although not appreciated by fellow servers or my supervisor, I can leave the room altogether. I'm a mess.

A week in, fellow wait-staff accuse me of stealing tips. Outraged by the accusation, livid that they would think me so terrible, I can find nothing to say to them, no warmth to dispel their distrust. My indignation only makes me colder and them more suspicious. I already hate the customers. Now, certain they don't like me, I hate my co-workers too.

My head waitress, a tall woman with an elaborate, braided hairpiece, takes it upon herself to bring me up to speed. She takes me home to her small apartment and introduces me to her five children. The rooms are bare but for small piles of random belongings. Her children run to greet her as she enters and she hugs them all, two dozen legs and arms gleefully entwined.

With kisses and hugs all around, she extricates herself, pulling bobby pins from her hairpiece as she does so, and shaking her own long braid free. Settling details with her spouse glimpsed briefly through the doorway, she waves goodbye, and we back out the door.

She takes us to a bar nearby on El Camino, where, once we are seated at the counter, she orders rum and Coke for both of us. The bartender sets the drinks down and I try mine. It's pretty good. She talks of the good life and love and family. I envy her and try to stay seated quietly at the bar, listening, appreciating.

But instead, I sip my drink through a blur of memory of the last time I tasted this concoction, its sweetness clinging to my clenched lips while I hung naked, tossing my head one way then the other, as monsters tried to make me drink it.

The memory makes this attempt at a simple after-work drink more nightmare than Happy Hour, but her efforts are well-intentioned, and I want to take them to heart. She wants to be friends, and I wish I knew how that felt.

Despite her best efforts at mentoring, I can't waitress now. I can't interact with all these people, look at their faces, or let them look at mine. The sounds in the restaurant roar in my head. The motion of customers, staff, and cooks blurs and confuses me, and I have nowhere to hide. There is no private space in a restaurant, and once on-shift, hiding out is not appreciated.

I wear out quickly and quit in an ugly fit, leaving a full station of rowdy customers waiting on post-game milkshakes and ice cream sundaes. Suddenly, I'm overwhelmed by the noise and color, and without thought except to escape, I set my loaded tray down on the floor in the midst of the room and leave the restaurant without a word to anyone.

I sit in BMP in the parking lot until the shaking subsides enough for me to drive away. Ashamed of my behavior, I never go back to the restaurant, and once again, forfeit my last paycheck. My breakdowns are expensive.

Unemployed once again, the idea of returning to school becomes more a goal and less a dream. I am a shadow who needs to keep busy and out of the way. School seems a good option. My social skills are reduced to zero, and I can't seem to hold a job, but sitting quietly in a classroom, this I think I can do.

I still need income, so this time I respond to an ad written on a three by five card and posted on a bulletin board at Foothill College. Without any harrowing interview, more just show up and begin, I'm hired to work as sales clerk in a small Sharon Heights gift shop. I do much better working with only one co-worker and one or two customers at a time, most of whom are older women. We try to be friends, the other sales girl and I, but we soon give it up. I can't find anything to say to her off the shop floor.

My new job leaves me enough time to go back to school, though not enough money. A scholarship and student loan close the gap. I enroll at Foothill and feel some hope that one dream may not be out of reach, that maybe I'm not ruined; maybe I can be fine, really.

I enroll in a full schedule and at first the anonymity of the classroom is soothing. I avoid contact with students or staff, and hurry between classes, work, and my own bedroom, the familiarity of the routine reassuring.

Unfortunately, my anthropology professor takes a shine to me. He invites me to join his student club, but I decline. I use lack of time as an excuse, though the truth is that gathering to chat with other students is out of the question. The very idea makes me break into a sweat. He is disappointed and assures me I have a future in the discipline. Ultimately, I drop the class, his attention quickly becoming unbearable.

Even with one class gone, I still have a full class schedule, having overbooked a little, and while I try to become a normal student, K works at the pool hall, where, when he isn't tending bar, he shoots pool and fleeces Stanford students of their stipends.

K's response to the Utah indignities has been to take up weightlifting and steroid abuse. He works out with our neighbor at the gym nearby and has bulked to enormous proportion.

Near the end of my first quarter at Foothill, a former resident of the Spaceship in Hawaii arrives on our doorstep unannounced, accompanied by his older brother.

K had reconnected with him during our brief and disappointing return to paradise, but the last we'd heard of his older brother, whom we have never met, he was wrapped in a bed sheet, hallucinating and running down the middle of Kalakaua Avenue. The next bit of story makes little sense as he recounts it now, but apparently Little Bro' rescued his elder, gave him more LSD in an effort to straighten him out, and has brought him to us for safekeeping.

Little Bro' promises us his older brother will be no trouble and needs to stay with us for only a few days. We say no, he can't stay; we have neither space nor time to watch over him.

Ignoring our attempts to decline, already retreating down the walkway, Little Bro' calls out an apology and promises, as he disappears around the corner, "I'll be back. Thanks!"

Elder Brother is large. He stands quietly on the doorstep, still clothed in a sheet, having adopted a John the Baptist look.

K has to leave for work. I have to study for finals. Scholarship money is on the line; I have to do well. K departs, and I try to be polite. I offer food and use of the facilities. He accepts both and emerges re-wrapped, now more Caesar than John.

The apartment is small, an entryway, living area, and a bedroom with no door. I offer more food and then attempt to go on about my business. I'm trying to study.

Big Brother seems simple, his speech slightly slurred, and his face bland. I have no idea if he was always so, or if this is a consequence of drug use, but he doesn't appear to be entirely present.

Although he is bathed and fed, within minutes it becomes obvious his one real need isn't yet met. He won't settle down and begins to loom. I know this posture, this feel. The vibe is unmistakable. Moving towards me, he quickly becomes too present.

I try to brush past him but he blocks my way.

Standing too close, looking down at me, he murmurs in a throaty whine, "I haven't been with a woman in a long time."

Not my problem, Brother.

By now, I am in full-flight, hysterical, frozen-woman status. As Brother compliments and attempts seduction, I relive horror, pain, disgust, and fury. Primarily fury, but my paralysis keeps him safe a moment longer.

He presses in, pinning me against the wall, "You're beautiful. I really need a woman."

He is coming on to me. I am fighting for my life. Mars and Venus square off.

My switch finally flips. I ram my knee into his crotch and shove him away with both hands as hard as I can. Neither effort gives him pause, and he seems surprised by my reaction. He also doesn't seem to recognize panic.

Fucking drug addicts.

The tears overflow and I can't speak, but I wrestle away from him and run to the kitchen phone, whirling in the numbers for K at work. Brother remains standing across the room, sputtering.

When I hear K's voice, I choke out the fear and beg him to please get this man out of here, to please help me. He promises help, and I hang up, cowering in the corner holding my breath, waiting for the world to end.

Moments later, the front door bangs open and five men burst in. K has called our weight-lifting neighbor and his fellow steroid-abusers at the gym. They've emptied the place and come to my rescue. Clad only in work-out shorts, the men overwhelm the room, taut-skin gleaming, beer-barrel thighs, tree-stump necks, each arm Thor's hammer.

They circle and stand shoulder to massive shoulder, facing bewildered Brother who now stands flattened against the wall, meager by comparison.

My huge protectors order him out, directing him to K's bar, where he can wait for his sibling to return. The men follow him to the street and stand guard until he has meandered out of sight, still shaking his head and muttering in confusion.

I earn the scholarship. Size does matter.

The Vietnam War comes to an end. Saigon falls. Returning vets are treated as if they are responsible for the disaster. Legal avenues to forgiveness for draft-evaders evolve.

With times changing, K decides to face his legal trouble. Living outside the law has worn him down. He returns to his home turf on the East Coast and hoping for leniency, turns himself in. Reflecting the mood of the country, he is convicted and spared prison, community service ordered instead. I don't see him again.

His absence widens the void between me and everything else. He was my connection to "before." He was the only one in my world who knew what happened, how it happened. He was the only one who knows who I was, who I am. The only one to whom I never owe an explanation or apology. My isolation wasn't so complete with him around. Now I hold onto only Beau for my life.

K takes his leave at the start of my next quarter at Foothill. With him gone, despite the scholarship and part-time cashier salary, I can't afford the apartment. I decide I have to go back to work full-time, and I drop out of school again, completing only one quarter.

For job-hunting this time, I find help from a neighbor and former middle-school friend, the last place I formed any real friendships. She lives close by, and we are trying to be friends again.

She arranges an interview for a position with the employment agency where she works. I arrive for my interview in full model regalia: false lashes, hair slicked back in a fashionable updo. I get the job, the office manager confident I will make an excellent first impression at the front desk.

In the intervening days, before I begin my new receptionist position, I see a hair stylist and we agree on a permanent for some curl and volume. My fine, straight hair does not take it well. The stylist is at a loss. No amount of cutting or shaping makes it presentable. My freak flag truly flies.

I arrive for my first day of work looking like a frightened Brillo pad. Nothing but time will fix it, and the manager is not pleased. This is not the face she hired, not the first impression she intended at her front desk. The hair softens somewhat, but she does not.

The tension remains palpable despite the fact that I am not bad at the job itself. My hair calms down, but I don't ever appear as polished as I had for the initial interview. The boss doesn't fire me but remains quite brusque. I feel a bit like I disappointed my mother.

Within a few months, I am saved from her disapproval by an opportunity to return to school. Little Sis invites me to move with her to Southern California. Having graduated from high school, she is headed to UC Irvine. Our stepfather is covering her living expenses, and I'm encouraged to join her. He'll subsidize my housing too, if I enroll in community college once there.

I decide to go. I need a way to survive. Fairly certain I won't last much longer as a receptionist; tagging along makes sense.

Beau stays behind with Big Sis. He and I have lived with her before. He'll have a big yard and a little pal. I know he's safe and well-loved, but I grieve his absence every moment and drive to and from LA many more times than truly necessary in order to hold him close.

Little Sis and I settle into a two-bedroom apartment on Balboa Island, not far from UC Irvine. I enroll at Orange Coast College, a bit farther down the way in Costa Mesa.

From our doorstep, the harbor, a jumble of gleaming and bobbing surfaces, glints in the distance. The indigo ocean stretches beyond our front door to infinity. We can almost hear waves. Human and auto traffic flow relentlessly along the beachfront. The breezes are warm and hospitable. Humanity and nature blend in a glow of competitive beauty.

But our surroundings go dreadfully underappreciated, the crowds keeping me inside and the burning sun, Little Sis. For the occasional evening out, we walk up the street to the Jolly Roger restaurant and enjoy hot fudge sundaes.

I am struggling to "get over it." I know I should be having fun, living the good life here in the heart of human opportunity. The chronic sunshine leaves no room for doubt in the goodness of life, but I remain under a cloud even here, somehow especially here. I don't remember what it feels like to want to do something for pleasure. I don't remember what it feels like to truly rest. I do what I have to do each day to survive—that's it.

Orange Coast College is a straight ride through Costa Mesa down Harbor Boulevard. Mile after mile of strip malls housing every conceivable effort to realize the American dream border both sides of the boulevard. Gaudy signs flash and rotate, offering sustenance, entertainment, and more signs. Commerce occupies every square inch of the endless sundrenched pavement.

By contrast, the college is as much park as campus. It has a familiar feel, much like Foothill or my high school, an architectural mixture of Spanish mission and Eichler.

I make immediate use of the campus career center. Finding entry-level jobs is becoming my specialty. With minimal human engagement, I'm allowed to scan the bulletin boards strewn with three by five cards for "no experience necessary" assignments. If they expect little, the interviews are easier. I present, at the most superficial level, as a reasonable human being.

I never take advantage of career planning—that would require meeting with someone to discuss myself and I don't want to do that—but I learn to find survival rations on my own, finding here a part-time job as copy clerk for a real estate developer.

The job offends me on many levels. I hate the work the company is doing, considering it rape of the land, and the men are smarmy, but I do the job well and keep my nausea to myself. I also keep the Gillette razor close at hand.

I enroll in a full schedule of classes for the semester but quickly drop the Native American Studies class when its professor explains we're required to present a project at the school fair. This is out of the question. I won't stand at a booth in public and chat with random passersby. I would rather die, but dropping the class is easier. It's an elective; I can lose it.

I try a science class. My background is minimal, and I hope to do better than I did as a younger student when my journal entries were never quite tidy enough for the teachers.

My science professor appears depressed and more than once refers to the professional life he might have had "if only…" It's clear that his role as teacher at a junior college does not qualify as success in his eyes. Having failed to meet his own standard, he muses aloud to us, his student audience, about despair and the ultimate purpose of life. The subject might be pertinent in some contexts, but we're studying the weather.

I am so unnerved by his melancholy that I report him to his department head. If he thought his life was in decline before, he hadn't yet heard me rant about him standing in front of a science class pondering his own potential suicide.

I dwell constantly on the thought myself, and I can't bear the sadness I hear in his voice. I want no encouragement to fall farther down my own tunnel. My compassion evaporated, instead of pity, I'm angry, unreasonable but sincere.

A new instructor appears at the next class session. I'm unstable, but articulate, and may have cost this man his job. I give up on science.

On the other hand, my World Literature instructor uses rock songs to illustrate her lectures and I love the class. She turns off the lights, and classmates lie on the floor letting Roberta Flack unite us by killing us softly. She lets me use half a class to recount the tale of Frankenstein as it is then unfolding on TV, for those among us who may have missed it. For a while, even Candide seems relevant.

Before the end of the semester at Orange Coast, I apply to UC Berkeley for undergraduate admission, and I'm accepted. I have patched together almost two years worth of credits and will enter a little shy of junior standing. Cal tuition is just under three hundred dollars, and I receive a grant. For food and books, I'm awarded work-study.

When I tell classmates I'm moving away, I'm surprised by how many of the males let me know they thought we would eventually hook-up. I'm at a loss as to why they think so. I'm friendly in class, I feel safe there, but I struggle with whom to present to the outside world.

My real self is a murderous, hateful monster that I keep coiled neatly, if not comfortably, in my belly. I pray for mass-extinction of our species. I want to be dead. I want everyone else to be dead. This monster occasionally spews out venom and puts me in danger. I try to control her, but she lurks just under the surface.

As an alternative, I cultivate the "too-nice-to-kill" persona, but realize here that this face is confusing and has created misunderstanding. Men don't realize my cheerful classroom-self doesn't exist beyond the classroom. I want to tell them to pretend I don't exist, but I don't. Outright rejection itself can be life-threatening.

Now, I realize I can't be pleasant but standoffish either, because it's taken as a challenge, a "she just hasn't said yes, yet." The best I can do is to avoid eye contact and let my body language discourage any approach: head down, keep moving.

I move off Balboa Island regretting how little I enjoyed it. Few places offer so many possibilities, but I am too withdrawn to take advantage of any of them: friendship, entertainment, a future. The regret sharpens my awareness of how crippled I feel.

Before leaving, I commit an act of malicious mischief, slicing my name into a wet cement curb in downtown Laguna Beach. The curb is painted red soon thereafter. I leave my mark in a No Parking zone.

CHAPTER 9

Not Meant to Last

Despite seeing no future and finding it hard to stand upright from the clench in my middle, I am overjoyed to be a UC Berkeley student. This is hallowed ground. I want to bow down on the steps in Sproul Plaza, though I never do. I walk quickly on, hoping no one can see me. In the temple of free speech, I have nothing to say, but I am thrilled to be here. The majesty of the place gives me hope that I might somehow find my voice.

University buildings dwarf the thirty thousand students attending with me. Some buildings are neo-classical homage, others architectural experiments. Campanile oversees all. The campus itself slopes gently toward the bay, crisscrossed with lawns and gravel pathways.

Bicycles, frisbees, the distinguished, and the lost swarm the paths. The air smells of falafel and pulses with the beat of djembe and bongos pounding out the rhythms of Berkeley life.

I move into a dorm on campus. It sits at a top corner of the university grounds. The stately brick building is ivy-covered and houses girls only. Inside, it harbors remnants of an elegant history. I mistakenly assume this will be a good fit for me.

I share a room with the only friendly resident I meet here. She is a local girl whose boyfriend sneaks in to join her in her twin bed most evenings. He may be very nice too. I try not to see him.

I feel very old in the other girls' presence. They seem to feel very superior in mine, though I'm aware that my perspective is off. I try not to take it personally, but the atmosphere is chill. Before long, the walk down the hall to the bathroom has me missing the more amiable atmosphere of drug addicts and prostitutes in the hotel hallway back in Denver.

For a brief while, I try. I ask about majors and hometowns to no avail. My presentation may be too dark. In line for breakfast one early morning, I remark in what I intend as an amusing tone to the bedraggled group surrounding me that we could be a line of women anywhere, even prison, given the way we look. None of the girls responds. Either no one hears me, or they don't appreciate the analogy.

It seems to me that the other girls sweep by, ignore my attempts at conversation or respond in dismissive tones, and I venture to the communal living area only once. The void between me and everyone else just feels too vast.

But that's okay girls, I don't like you either.

I go home to Palo Alto each weekend and stay with Beau in my familiar garage. He's a big dog now, and my anchor to the world. I don't know why I'm so miserable, but here in the garage, my face nestled against his soft black fur, I find enough incentive to keep at it anyway.

My first class at Cal is a night class. I arrive early. My knees are shaking as I pull open the class door. I was comfortable at community college, but here I'm intimidated by the ivy and stone. I want to be up to this. I want to fit in.

The classroom is small, not the vast theater I expect. The professor, a bantam rooster, preens at the lectern as the room fills to overflowing. He makes his introduction and welcomes his returning students from the first quarter class.

Class begins. He struts and lectures, and at what seems like an appropriate moment, I raise my hand. The professor has taken questions cordially so far, and I have no reason to suspect I will not be well-received. However, I ask how he is defining the "foundations of literature" to which he keeps referring, and his splutter makes clear just how ignorant I am. He responds by asking a fellow classmate who *has* attended his first quarter class, to *enlighten* me.

I'm so embarrassed by the condescension that I have to escape. Tears hovering, lips clenched to stop the chin quiver, I stand up in the midst of the class-pet's recital, shoulders back, chin high, and march out of the room, letting the door slam closed behind me. I hate everyone. I want to kill myself. I can't believe I just did that.

I drop the class. My others are large lectures, and I never ask another question.

My shame is so complete now that I have trouble standing up. My stomach hurts all the time. I can't bear to be looked at. I hunch over and keep my eyes down, scurrying from class to class, and hiding in-between.

On campus, finding a private, safe place to hide is difficult. My dorm room is too far away, and the usual haunts where students loiter, untenable.

The ladies' rooms are too public and too gross.

The plazas are out of the question, too many people moving in too many directions. I can't follow the action well enough to keep myself safe. Eye contact and physical contact is inevitable, I dread both. I can pass through, but not linger.

The library is treacherous with its close labyrinths where I could be easily trapped. I suspect the male students go out of their way to brush past between the narrow bookshelves. The study corrals can hide me, but they're too far inside the labyrinth. The building is too open, too close, and too public. I don't go in unless driven by inescapable, academic need.

The cafeteria is complex, and choosing a safe place to sit leaves me conspicuous for too long. For the food, I have to stand in line next to fellow students who have no idea how revolting their casual brushes against me feel as they grab for the offerings around us, and I have to make eye contact with the serving staff, letting them see me. The noise and motion in the room make me vibrate, and someone might ask to sit with me. I go in only once. After that the cafeteria too, is off limits.

I fantasize about walking downtown on Shattuck Avenue and strolling among the saffron-robed Krishna monks, sharing the chant for a few minutes before moving on to buy falafel from a sidewalk cart. But the same longing I knew in Waikiki, when being cool was my highest goal, fails me. Now I'm too afraid of everyone, even Krishna monks, to give it a try.

Between classes this first quarter, twice a week, I hide in the lecture hall where my next class will eventually convene. I arrive as the previous class is departing, and I take my chosen seat in the large lecture hall to wait in the quiet theater for the hour before my own class begins.

Each day when I enter, the lecturer for the previous class is at the podium, collecting his notes before descending the stairs and leaving the lecture hall. He's young, perhaps a TA, serious and tall. I notice him because he is invariably the last to leave, and once he's gone, for a while I have the still room, blessedly, to myself.

A few weeks in, the TA descends the stairs but rather than leave, he walks over and sits down beside me. I stop breathing, planning my escape, considering my attack.

"I don't mean to be forward," he says as he proceeds to be, "but I see you come in, and you always look so sad. Is there anything I can do?"

His eyes sear me with their compassion, kindness slashes as if lethal. Pain wells up, my throat constricts. *Where would I begin?* Short of inflicting amnesia, what could possibly be done?

I choke out a "Thanks, but..." as I dissolve into tears and leap from my seat. I may have knocked him and his best-of-intentions from his own, as I fly away. I add the shame that total strangers can see I am not "over it" to my list of failures. I walk naked. I can't even pretend to be all right.

I stop using the room as my hideout and sit on a bench in another building instead. I pray I will never see the TA again, but do wish I were brave enough to apologize and to thank him for his concern.

At the end of classes, with summer beginning, I give up the dorm room and move back to the garage in Palo Alto. Beau, the privacy, and good final grades soothe and settle me.

With school out, I have to find summer work. I should have enough work history to move ahead somewhat by now, but the circumstances of my leaving prior jobs contain enough humiliation to insure that I have no references to speak of and little experience I want to mention.

Heading again to the familiar, I search for work on the bulletin board in the student career center and find the perfect job posted on a familiar three by five card—flexible hours, no experience necessary.

The ad is looking for cocktail waitresses for the Red and White Fleet tourist boats sailing from Fisherman's Wharf. Aside from the rum and coke, I have never had a cocktail, nor ever been in an actual bar, except for the one visit with my head waitress, but if I have to work somewhere, this job sounds like fun. I desperately want something to be fun.

I apply at the Fleet office and am once again hired on the spot. The fact that I know nothing of cocktails is never mentioned.

I report for work at the small office shack near the Ferry Terminal. The Red and White boats jostle their docks in the water alongside. As directed, I find my assignment on a clipboard hanging on the wall and pretend to fit right in.

At night, the boats are rented out for parties and I serve cocktails. It takes me a little while to learn the ropes. Customers order drinks with names I can't pronounce, and service is a bit confused at the start. I drop several beer and champagne bottles on my own head trying to hold them on trays above the crowded dance floor before I get my balance and learn how to serve drinks at sea. But the atmosphere is cordial, the music loud, and I'm surrounded by protective deck hands.

We host a hoedown one night and the next, the organizers of the Fourth Annual Freedom Day Parade. I learn a bit about my fellow human beings watching them get loose on the ocean: some have terrible taste in music, and some unexpected souls can really dance.

Weekdays, I work the tour boats that carry visitors out into the Bay. I stand behind the candy counter and sell souvenirs. The bark of sea lions, cry of gulls, and cold winds sweeping through the Golden Gate freshen my dark spirits. The eternity of the ocean reminds me I am still alive.

Before long, I learn that the regular Fleet servers are on strike and that I am a scab. After an informative confrontation with a genuine and rather formidable cocktail waitress, I quit. The first and only time I regret having to do so.

For the next school year, I stay in the garage in Palo Alto and commute to Berkeley. The long commute is brutal, but I would rather spend time in travel than live with strangers.

My commute options are two, both taking just under two hours: driving across the San Mateo Bridge and then north on to Berkeley, or crossing the Dumbarton Bridge to Hayward to catch BART—our new Bay Area Rapid Transit.

When underway, BART is a marvel—just like Disneyland—but when it is not, which in this early stage is often, patience is required. Travel times vary.

The trains are new, the tracks new, the wiring new. Rain stops us. Unknown forces stop us. We travel inexplicably backwards, passing wanted stops, occasionally ordered to disgorge at unwanted ones. Sometimes the train pulls in, never opens its doors, then pulls away, leaving those waiting for it gazing longingly at the receding cars, clinging to the optimist's hope that another train will appear. And one will, eventually.

I have little patience or spare time; after a few attempts with the future, I drive BMP.

I'm awarded work-study and find a job in the Financial Aid office. I know a lot about the subject, financial aid being a staple of my survival tools, and I can relate to students. My office demeanor is too-nice-to-kill. I bubble. I am shamelessly obsequious.

The office director, a modest woman who spends summers at the Shakespeare Festival in Ashland, tells me I am the best student to ever work for her, and pens a lovely reference letter that she tells me not to mention to anyone because she will not write one for anyone else. I hold the letter in the ladies' restroom and cry all over it, smearing whatever it says. Beyond class essays and final exams, I haven't done anything well in a long time.

The downside to the oh-so-helpful Ms. Sunshine I present to the office director is that I annoy my co-worker. She takes to calling me Ms. La Di Da until she realizes that she's hurt my feelings, that her opinion matters to me.

She becomes a friend, my first in a long time. A single mother with an enormous heart, her friendship brings me outdoors. We hike to Pt. Reyes and wander in Muir Woods, dwarfed and shaded by the ancient redwoods. Her mother and I lug a picnic cooler between us as she shepherds her daughter, and Beau bounds alongside.

We stay friends for a little while, until once again the attempt at friendship makes me feel even more isolated, different and wrong; the gap between me and everyone else just too vast for me to cross.

With the new quarter underway, as I get used to my new class schedule, I begin to feel compelled to sit in approximately the same place in each classroom, finding the analog in every layout. Not too near the front—too conspicuous. Not too far back—too difficult to pay attention. Not on the end—too much contact with other students. And always, egress within sight. It becomes very important for me to know exactly where I am headed at all times, door to door.

Then, for several days in a row, I can't manage to sit through my classes. I think I'm listening but miss whole sections of lectures. After a few minutes, I struggle to breathe, and I can't sort out what I hear. Several times, I have to leave the room during class. Once outside, I need to huddle somewhere small, but there is nowhere. I spend class hours disoriented in the hallway trying to just not be anywhere for a little while. I still cannot disappear at will, and I do so need this particular superpower.

Afraid that I'm losing the ability to do the one thing that I was sure I could do—be a student—I turn once more to a doctor for help. I make an appointment at the student medical center. When the voice on the phone asks me why I want to make an appointment, I don't know what to say; that in itself is a part of the problem. I choose to say depression. It's easier to explain and seems an appropriate place to start.

I arrive for the appointment and meet in a small cubicle with a staff psychiatrist who is pregnant enough to cause me some worry.

We don't connect. Her still face and calm stare whisper disinterest. She asks why I'm there. I rattle through the rape, fighting my own internal hum that intensifies as I speak, making it increasingly difficult to stay seated. I may levitate but am concentrating too hard on finishing the story to check.

I conclude with a description of being asked to return for a polygraph test. I laugh through the end, the humiliation complete.

She stares, unsmiling, and responds after only a breath, "You do realize laughter is inappropriate?"

The way I tell it? That's where I'm going wrong?

I hear nothing else she says or that I say. Her observation may be true, but it hits me as cutting and cruel. I don't like her and don't care what else she has to say. I would like to tell her she needs to work on her bedside manner, but I'm silenced. Not only am I failing to "get over it," now I'm not even telling it right.

She doesn't seem to appreciate how limited my emotional range is just now. I want to scream at her to find out what emotion she would find appropriate in this collegiate, semi-private space. Shall I throw something? Sob? Curse? Does she offer someone I might beat up? Once again, no response seems appropriate. I begin to wonder if any ever will.

I don't schedule another appointment. Insightful criticism is not helpful.

I find smaller niches near my classrooms and learn to cope. I cry alone in my garage bedroom and stay as far away from everyone and everything as possible. The school year passes in a haze of driving, reading, and writing. I do well enough in my classes.

As summer approaches and work-study ends, I go to work as a hostess in the Bullock's department store coffee shop and move to Walnut Creek with a family friend for my final year at Cal. I am numb, but cordial.

We see the freeway from the front porch, but the rent is reasonable. We have a yard for Beau, and the commute to school is under twenty minutes.

My roomie and I know each other through older siblings. We were only a year apart in high school and almost remember each other. He doesn't frighten me; I know his family. We settle into a comfortable, platonic routine, like the old friends we almost are.

At work in the upscale café, I join a close-knit group. The manager is good, and I hope to be a team member. When one of the servers needs temporary care for his five-foot-long boa constrictor, Julius Squeezer, I volunteer. We had a smaller boa as a pet when I was young; they're fascinating.

Julius is delivered with his enormous aquarium, heater, and lamps. His owner assures me he won't need to be fed—he just ate—and that he'll return for Julius in a week.

Within a few hours of his having been left with me, I hear what sounds like rasping from the huge snake. Repeatedly opening his jaws wide, he seems to be struggling to breathe. I'm sure he's ill. I try my best to find his owner, but the boy is on vacation, off the grid.

This snake cannot die on my watch, better that I do, than him. Looking for help, I telephone a familiar vet in Palo Alto. He refers me to a university doctor in New York. His office refers me to an expert in Canada. As I'm struggling with scenarios of how I will travel across country with the enormous sick serpent, this vet refers me to a practitioner right down the road.

In a serendipitous turn, a top expert in reptile healthcare practices in my backyard, his office only a few miles away. I call his clinic and describe what I've seen. They tell me to bring Julius right in; they fear he's in mortal danger.

I have only to drive a few exits down the freeway, but I'm stumped as to how to travel with Julius even this distance. He has to be kept warm. The weather is cold, BMP has no heater, and his terrarium is too big for the back seat.

I decide my best option is to rest him wrapped around my shoulders underneath my thick wool cardigan, a souvenir from Mexico. He can have my body warmth, and I'll know exactly where he is.

Once wrapped, Julius rests cooperatively, draped over my shoulders. His weight takes some getting used to. I slip the sweater over both of us and ease into BMP's driver's seat. Julius settles in, his scales rippling against my neck as a slow undulation flows the length of his body, his coils now a little tighter.

I back out of the driveway and onto the nearby 680 freeway ramp, easing into heavy, afternoon traffic. Shifting gears, we speed up. Julius ripples again, tighter still, now more coiled around my neck than draped on my shoulders. I feel my pulse beating against his belly.

I find his head and work my fingers around, trying to loosen him. He ripples again. I wriggle my index finger down between his belly and my throat, trying to wedge some space between his scales and my skin. He snugs my fingers into his embrace.

Maneuvering through traffic, watching for the exit, steering and shifting gears with one hand while the other slides back and forth trying to loosen the snake, I start to worry. I can't budge him—not in commute traffic while driving a stick shift. For any unwinding I do, he adjusts with the sinuous ripple. Blood flow is slowing, and I'm beginning to see stars.

As I wrestle with Julius, I glance out the side window and notice that travelers in cars around me are in uproar, drivers waving and gesturing, eyes wide, hands over mouths, children crying. Apparently, I appear to be under attack by a giant snake. I suppose they couldn't possibly imagine that I intentionally left the house with it wrapped around my neck.

Trying to put the audience at ease by smiling and nodding at everyone, I continue driving with one hand and avoiding strangulation with the other until the turnoff appears. I exit, leaving my fellow travelers to puzzle over what they've actually seen as we pass from sight.

The vet's office is very near. I do my best to keep a finger wedged between my carotid artery and Julius as I stagger inside. He feels much heavier now that I haven't had a decent breath in several minutes.

As I come in, vet staff shriek in alarm and leap to my aid, grabbing various snake lengths. It takes three people to unwind him. Once my vision clears, I am fine, really, just embarrassed.

After Julius is treated—a shot of antibiotics does it—the expert delivers a stern lecture telling me this is the single most stupid thing he has ever seen anyone do.

"Do you have any idea how big this snake is?"

Well, yes. Now I do.

I'm certain Julius had no ill intention, merely seeking a warmer ride, but I don't mention it. The vet seems quite flustered.

They provide a padded box for the trip home and suggest I turn up his heat lamp. Julius survives, but his owner sticks me with the vet bill.

CHAPTER 10

Leave It If I Please

Until now, I've gone to school in random fashion. I have no academic goal; school is my cover. As a student, I appear to be a worthwhile human being engaged in a worthwhile activity, while in truth I am merely leaping from one hiding place to another, my long-term plans nonexistent. I see no future, being still inordinately distracted by the past.

Each new day is an unwelcome miracle. Knowing what awful potential it holds, I can't imagine preparing to live through very many of them. Each night, I debate choosing to live through one more. But despite my reluctance, the days continue to come and go and my class credits add up. Graduation looms on the horizon; decisions must be made.

Beyond delusions of grandeur, I can't imagine what practical use I will make of a degree. I have studied across disciplines, exploring problems facing developing countries, still wishing I could save the world (I thought we had handled that in an earlier decade, but apparently something more than love is required, or there just is not yet enough of it), but have no further plan.

In what remains of me, I dream of going on for an advanced degree, but I consider it beyond reach. I've made no connections with professors who might write letters of recommendation. The few conversations I've been forced to engage in have been brief, awkward, or horrifying. And beyond no human connections, I have no resources to finance such a dream.

With the growing fear of "What next?" chewing at me, I accept that I need help finding a direction, and looking for it, I head to the Quonset hut that serves as the counseling center for Cal students. I hope to walk in and to take vocational and aptitude tests. I need a plan for my afterlife.

Instead of my bustling in and taking tests, I am given an appointment to return in three weeks. When I arrive for this appointment, I am greeted by a young woman who leads me down a long hall to a small office with a desk and two chairs. Sun shines in the small window. It looks as much like a M.A.S.H. set inside the hut as outside. My escort smiles, gestures to the vacant chair. and closes the door behind her. Seated in the other chair behind the desk is a chubby-faced psych grad student who introduces himself and begins asking me questions.

I am immediately hysterical, despite appearing to be sitting completely still. I cannot be in this tiny space with this stranger, this man. I am in so much danger I can't believe the sun hasn't blown up.

How dare you? I'm here to take tests, not share my life story with a child who knows nothing about anything.

I reiterate to him that I am here to take tests. He reiterates that he would like some background.

No, you don't. My background is none of your business.

"I'm here to take the tests."

We exchange stares.

He sighs, scratches some notes, and puts down his pencil.

We schedule the tests. I am to return to take them in three weeks.

When the time comes, I take the battery—lots of "What would you choose?" and "How do you feel?"

I pretend I feel something and care about something too, but I don't know what it is. When the tests are finished, I'm told to come back in three weeks to pick up the results. I schedule the appointment.

When I return to pick up my results, again I am escorted to the office where Mr. Grad Student is seated behind the desk with a stack of papers, my test results, in front of him. I ask to have them.

He says no, he is to go over the results with me. He'll help me "interpret them."

I say no, I haven't the time. I will take my results and review them myself.

He says no again.

My boiling point is low. I started out being put off by his gender, now it is by his personality as well.

He suggests we schedule another time to go over them if I haven't the time right now.

I say no, the results are mine and I want them.

My voice rises, "Do you have any idea how long it takes to make an appointment here? I'm going to graduate before I get the fucking results."

I boil over a bit.

He responds, "You must have been very deprived as a child to work so hard to make people reject you."

He is lucky he lives through his textbook observation; I explode. I have the impression I hit the reed top of the hut but may just smash its sides, crashing through something and roaring down the hallway, shrieking obscenities. and demanding to see the director of this miserable fucking program. Storming through a door with Director written on it, I spew indignation and fury around the room at an assortment of bewildered faces until I can shriek no more.

Backing out of the room, sobbing, I run blindly through the building until I find an exit and slam through it, hurling hatred into the world outside with each ragged breath.

The unmanageable hurt makes no sense to me, but apparently he hit a nerve.

As I spew venom, other students glide by, cutting an arc on the path around me, minding their own business. I am just one of many odd characters wandering about, only somewhat more vitriolic than most at the moment.

I never return to the counseling center. No one follows up. I never find out what the tests revealed except for the two results Mr. Grad Student mentioned as he tried to persuade me to sit down. I scored 99 on being an army officer and negative 3 on mortician.

I tried to cheat the tests but they found me out: I really want nothing to do with death, and I want to be in charge, heavily armed, even better.

I give up on making a plan and instead submit graduation paperwork to both departments in which I've earned enough credits to graduate, leaving the next step undefined.

The Walnut Creek house where Beau and I spend my final months at Cal is a safe haven. My roommate didn't stay in school very long, but remains a roommate anyway. His friends come and go, and he bonds with a neighbor across the street. This neighbor works for the Red Cross.

One evening, Mr. Red Cross brings home a young runaway who has been raped, sheltering her until her transport home can be arranged. There are no females in his immediate world, so he asks if I will come over and sit with her. He thinks I might be of comfort.

I'm very uncertain that I have anything soothing to offer, but I agree to give it a go, and follow him back across the street. He opens his front door and I see a young girl sitting quite still at the kitchen table, her hands folded around the cup she stares into.

I can't go inside. I look at her and can't think of any way I could be helpful. My killer instinct is not soothing. I want to scream. I want to rip every living soul within reach to shreds.

What could I say to her? I won't insult her with platitudes. I can tell her to go on, to keep breathing, but can't offer any hope that she won't be sick to her stomach with fear for the rest of her life. Better to say nothing, I won't help her dig that hole.

I pull back from the doorstep before she sees me. Unable to utter a sound, shaking my head, I stumble back across the street into the safety of my own tiny black hole, leaving my Good Samaritan neighbor standing at the door watching me flee, speechless and seemingly bewildered by my flight. I assume he thinks me beneath contempt for refusing to help. I agree with him. I can't even summon compassionate courage.

Once back in the safety of my own room, I unwrap the razor blade and slash my wrists for the first time in a while, adding a few smashes with the hammer handle to my arms and legs for good measure, wishing again that the men had killed me; I'm so useless.

But still, I do not check out. I love Beaujangles and he needs me. I do what I can do. I go to class, go home, read, and go back to class. I seat customers at the restaurant and take their money. I ignore my upcoming graduation and stick to my routine.

My roommate's life keeps me connected to the wider world (no one says anything about my failure with the girl) and as winter passes, one of his friends offers to teach me to ski.

I imagine a skier's life as perfect: active, outdoors, free. I'm excited. I aspire to the insouciance of ski bum, picturing a life in Lake Tahoe where I might finally be cool. He promises to teach me at Kirkwood Meadows over spring break.

I have skied only once before, when I was fifteen, and I may bear responsibility for another child breaking her leg, though I can't be sure—the scene was rather chaotic. I hope to do better this time.

When the scheduled weekend arrives, he and I leave for Lake Tahoe in the early evening. Traffic into the Sierras is heavy, but the weather is good, the Milky Way is strewn above us, and the Hunter's Belt follows us all the way.

We pull in to Kirkwood near midnight. Floodlights bathe the mountainside. "Free Bird" blares from lodge speakers. Skiers swarm down the gleaming mountain, Lynyrd Skynyrd egging them on. They fly, agile and reckless, over the giant moguls and into the night sky.

I can't wait to learn to ski.

Early the next morning, we visit the lodge shop, and I am outfitted in rental equipment. Once appropriately encased, I flail along behind my newfound friend turned ski instructor, out of doors. I trudge in spastic, forward thrusts—he glides—to a little hill. We spend time here as I learn to stay upright, and then we move on to more complicated things. Finally, I snow plow, plant, and turn to his satisfaction. He pronounces me ready.

Once again, I flail along beside him until we reach the chair lift where I am successfully caught up without humiliation or loss.

The day is gorgeous: a powder-blue sky, the sun bright, the air cool, the snow crisp and quick.

We ride to the top of the mountain. Kirkwood Lodge peeks through in the distance below, miniature, far, far away.

As we approach the top, I panic and leap off the chairlift too soon. My friend leaps after me, shoving me away from the next set of skis sailing over, and we stagger to our feet unharmed for my first real day of skiing, off to a disturbing start.

We stand at the crest of the mountain looking over the lip where the wind blows the snow in a perpetual fog up into the sky on even this beautiful sunny day. So far, skiing is terrifying.

My teacher assures me I will do fine. "Just do what you did on the little hill," he offers cheerfully.

It was easier when there was no risk of plummeting to my death, but okay. Shaking from both fear and cold, I have no choice. Like childbirth, only way out is down.

We begin crisscrossing the steep wall, gently losing altitude. He swishes one direction then the other, calling his instructions and corrections as he passes, his voice rising in impatience as I make little progress. He leaps and twirls around me. Other skiers swoosh past.

I travel a foot or two and fall. I get up, travel another foot and fall. I get up. I fall. It isn't very much fun.

Not long into this frustrating attempt to teach me to ski, several of my teacher's friends hail him from the lift passing overhead. Hot skiers, once off the lift they quickly sweep in around us, jostling, joking, sharing cocaine.

I decline; it makes me nervous.

They circle about, laughing and offering encouragement until, having sufficiently shaken the world around them, they swoop off.

My teacher watches them grow tiny in the distance.

I feel guilty. I'm a terrible student, and I know he wants to enjoy the perfect day. He isn't much help anyway; falling down a mountainside is a solitary pursuit. I tell him to go ahead.

"You sure?"

Are you insane?

"Yeah, I'll find you at the bottom." I feign confidence that I will one day reach the bottom.

"You're doing great. Just do what we practiced." His voice trails after him as he too, swoops away with a bird's grace, free at last.

Cocaine is not your friend.

I stand a moment in the sky and look down. It's a long way to go, one tumble at a time.

A few meters later, I rip off the rental skis and hurl them off the cliff beside me.

I reach the bottom by late afternoon, numb from exhaustion, cold, and disappointment. When it comes up, I tell him where they can find the skis.

The real damage however, I do to myself. I remain outside in the sun and snow glare all day without sunscreen; my entire face blisters. I not only fail to learn to ski or even to enjoy it, but within hours, I can't open my eyes or close my lips.

The pain is excruciating and healing takes weeks. I begin my last quarter at Cal appearing to have an untreated case of leprosy. I don't meet with any advisors or make any friends this final quarter either.

In June of 1976, I graduate from Berkeley, proud and exhausted. I cry through my graduation ceremony and toss my cap into the air with everyone else.

I haven't learned the names of any of my fellow thirty-thousand students or approached any instructors. A piece of paper is all the evidence I have that I was there. It will have to do.

I'm awarded two bachelor's degrees with distinction—one in Political Science and one in Economics. I suspect I really only earned one but don't object. I tried first to turn in my graduation paperwork in the Poli Sci office where the secretary was so curt that I left the papers but abandoned hope of finishing anything with her. I tried instead in the Econ office and was greeted warmly enough. Both departments end up issuing degrees, and I don't argue. *Why not two?* I worked hard.

Two degrees or no, I still have no direction. I studied what interested me but can't imagine myself in the world beyond. I'm afraid to enter anyone's office but wish I could; I have questions.

The lease for the Walnut Creek house is up. My roommate plans to move on. I need a plan.

Forced to make a move—I want only to curl into a ball and be still—I accept an offer from my roommate's friends to share space with them in South Lake Tahoe. Beau is welcome too, and it should be easy to find restaurant work, the only experience I find useful. Servers earn enough to survive, maybe even to relax, and I don't have to ski.

The Tahoe house holds a small community, the residents numerous enough that I'm never quite sure to whom I owe my gratitude. The air is crisp, the forest quiet, and everyone means to have a good time. The vibe is very Waikiki. I find a spare room and hope the atmosphere will lift my spirits.

Needing to find work right away, I set up interview appointments with casino HR's, arriving for my first scheduled appointment at Harvey's where I am hired as a coffee shop waitress. I decline the initial offer to serve as a cocktail waitress, not that confident, but accept the alternative food service position. I'm sure I can wait tables now. I'm fine, really. I'm a college graduate.

The HR lady sits at her desk behind a glass partition. She leans her blond bouffant forward and asks if I can begin right away.

I'm stunned at the idea. I want to shout "No!" I need to go away and think about it first, but I'm fairly certain the offer depends upon my showing up right now.

"Yeah. That would be fine!" I strive for sincerity.

"Great!" She does too.

Ms. HR turns around and in Spanish asks the young girl who is currently emptying the wastebasket behind her to take me to the coffee shop and to hand me off to the shift supervisor.

The girl nods and leads me out onto the casino floor. I follow her into the flashing cavern of slots and tables that stretches endlessly ahead of us. Exits are nowhere to be seen. Bells clash, people and cigarette smoke swirl.

I have never spent time in a casino, merely passing through a few times in days past to take advantage of the cheap buffet inside. Then they looked like fun, now I'm not sure.

I follow my escort into the coffee shop, passing under the longhorns spanning its entrance. She presents me to a tall man who is delighted to meet me. He bubbles that they need help on the floor right away.

"Great to meet you! Get a uniform and come right back. We'll get you squared away." He asks the young girl to show me where the uniforms are handed out.

"Great to meet you," he calls again over his shoulder as he bustles off.

I am fighting the shock. I am not ready. This isn't a good idea. The room is so big. Everyone is moving so fast.

I fight with my competing needs: one to freeze to a stop and the other to run as fast and as far away as I can—the reality and my limitations in head-on collision. This is not how I do things. This is too sudden. I haven't had any chance to talk myself out of all the terrible things that might happen. I need to mull this over. I have to GET READY.

My escort, oblivious to my rising panic, leads me to the back of the restaurant—behind counters, through doors, down stairs and hallways dotted with doorways leading to small spaces, down more stairs.

As we wind farther and farther down, my blind hysteria wells up.

She leads me through a door and asks the clerk inside for a coffee shop uniform. He checks me out, figuring a size.

I'm shaking, my teeth chattering. The girl's voice is too loud, both too far away and too close. The path down here has undone me. I don't understand why, but I am flying around the ceiling. The clerk hands me a pile of clothes. His arms stretched too far, from too far away. I take them but can only stare at them, I can't speak.

I turn to my escort and manage to straighten my arms enough to offer them to her.

She stares.

I choke out, "You take it."

She grimaces, I'm making no sense.

"The job."

I unwind. Tears overwhelm me and I can't form any more words. My middle collapsing, I shove the uniform at her, and she takes it rather than let it drop to the floor, still staring at me, bewildered.

I try to explain, but the words are trapped in sobs and my own confusion.

Giving up, I flee the room, running down halls and up stairways until I find an emergency exit and slam through it. I can't breathe, and I don't know where I am. I walk blind, choking back convulsive tears, fighting to catch my breath.

Finally, I unclench enough to walk like a normal person and to get my bearings. I reach a familiar parking lot and find my trusted BMP, hiding inside her until I can breathe and see well enough to drive away.

Back at the commune, I don't tell anyone that I blew a perfectly good job.

The next morning, I try again. I present myself across the street at Harrah's HR department, the appointment already scheduled. I hadn't cancelled it before losing my mind the previous afternoon.

I'm furious with myself for throwing away a job, but I have recovered enough to convince myself that it was the coffee shop itself. I just didn't like it there. I think it was the longhorns. I now have it under control. I am fine, really.

Once more in full façade, I present myself and my paperwork at the Harrah's HR window. For a moment the bespectacled, grey-haired lady seated behind it measures me over the top of her glasses. She reviews the papers in front of her once more before scribbling across the bottom. She tells me the interview is cancelled.

"Unstable," she says as she hands the papers back to me. Eighteen hours after my meltdown, I am unemployable in South Lake Tahoe.

CHAPTER 11

Waiting Longer

I leave Lake Tahoe and return to more familiar territory, finding an apartment to share in Redwood City, an in-law unit behind a family home. Roommates come and go.

In this, our country's bi-centennial year, jobs are not difficult to come by. The surrounding valley's farms and orchards, the best agricultural land on earth, is being eagerly cemented over with opportunities.

Fireworks are also in large supply.

I abandon food service as a career option. Not sure why, but I can no longer handle it. I fail even to get the uniform on this last time. I need another new plan.

Contact with people is exhausting. I can't trust my composure, and I can't meet anyone's eyes. The model façade holds up, but I know that behind it, I'm grotesque, beyond inspection. The interrogation that accompanies job-hunting may as well be public execution.

I find a position with help again from the kind-hearted girl friend who helped me once before. Now working on Page Mill Road for a company giving birth to both the biotech industry and creative financing, she doesn't hold the bad permanent against me and offers another bootstrap.

Headquarters for the company is a new brick building with sweeping staircases, oak-studded lawns viewed through walls of plate glass windows, and a free cafeteria for employees and their guests. Good digs.

The enthusiastic HR director is certain they can use me. I have two bachelor degrees and should make great support staff for someone. I am pliant and have experience with this and that, if no career direction. My ambition extends only so far as finding my next foxhole.

She sends me around the company to audition. I'm rejected by marketing executives, but the new VP of legal services loves me.

HR is initially reluctant to send me to interview with him because he is reputed to be "very difficult." She lowers her voice with the observation. He has lost two secretaries in quick succession, a bad sign. But I'm game. I need a job and the place is clean.

The new VP is nervous and doesn't know when to stop talking, seemingly uncomfortable with his new success, but he's smart and funny, and I like him right away. I understand it—he's funny when he's afraid.

Again, I'm hired immediately. He admits he's supposed to discuss it with HR before he offers me the job, but he knows it's fine. I'm in.

I buy five dresses at Bullocks in Stanford Shopping Center and show up for work in my favorite one the following Monday. My desk sits outside my boss's office.

I get off to a good start with the secretary next to me. She's friendly and shows me how to turn on my typewriter.

Soon after I'm hired, executives begin a betting pool on which of them will "nail the new talent first." This is tradition among them. One of the bettors lets me know about it. I'm not sure whether or not to thank him for the disclosure.

Could this be more awkward?

The ritual for "new talent" also includes an initial inspection by the company founder's chauffeur. Within days of my arrival, he visits my workspace, meandering to my desk, picking up and examining random items and shooing away my inquiries as to how I might help him. He appears to be lame, ill-tempered, and lost, but I discover not the latter, at least.

If the chauffeur ranks new talent hot enough, the man himself soon wanders by.

Apparently, I pass the pre-screen. Within a few days, the dapper, elder gentleman himself, the company's namesake, saunters by with a glance at me on his way into my boss's office—my boss is not in. The office door clicks closed and, a moment later, my phone rings; he's calling me from my boss's phone.

I may have passed the appearance portion of the test but apparently fail the personality segment. The phone conversation is stilted, pointless, and brief. I learn later from other "talent" of its point. Had I impressed him, a rendezvous in the chauffeured vehicle would have been suggested.

Once the company alpha male passes, the other men are free to continue their contest. Before I'm told about it and stop falling for the ruses, the competitive attention takes many forms.

Beside my desk, I have tacked a poster to the wall: seagulls soar through cloudy skies. The inscription reads, "They can, because they think they can."

One afternoon, I find a note on my desk that reads, "They think they can, because they can." The observation is from a scientist whose office is across the hall, obviously not a Norman Vincent Peale enthusiast.

A few days later, the author of the note invites me to lunch. At noon, he crosses from his office to my desk and presents himself. He is mid-west button-down, wrapped in his usual white lab coat.

"Plans for lunch?"

He catches me off guard. I did not realize the dose-of-reality note was a prelude. My moment's surprised hesitation lasts long enough to require the truth.

"No."

"Join me?"

I may as well be thirteen-years-old. My heart pounds and I demand my legs prepare to stand up and follow this perfectly nice man to his car. We are going for lunch. One hour. How difficult can this be? Grow up. GET OVER IT.

"Yeah, sure."

We stroll out to the parking lot, and he opens his car door for me; stepping in takes all my will. I slide onto the seat just the way my eighth grade gym teacher taught us at Terman Junior High, letting us practice by getting in and out of her Alpha Romeo parked behind the tennis courts.

He does not say very much. I twitter, sampling small talk to little avail. We back out of the parking space and through the lot in a slightly awkward silence.

As we pull onto El Camino, he casually mentions, "I have to stop at my house first."

More observer than participant, I pretend to be riding in this car although I'm actually far away, floating elsewhere, but I hear him, and my alarm level ratchets up.

To myself, I get harsh, "*GET REAL. BE HERE NOW.*" I am trying.

To him, "No problem." I lie.

He pulls into his driveway, and he invites me in.

"Only a minute." Now he lies.

I follow him. *"How many times can lightning strike?"* I repeat to myself as I follow this man into his home.

He waves me to the seating and says he'll be right back, disappearing down the hall. I look around. It's a bachelor's home but very orderly. I wonder if he's a tad OCD.

I'm admiring his bookshelf when he emerges from the hallway carrying two bathrobes. He tosses them casually over the back of the couch, smiling at me.

I use the best defense I have and laugh it off, mocking the insulting assumption as I back out of the house. I go back to the car, and if we have lunch, I don't remember it.

I'm fine, really.

Others are less direct. I am instructed via memo to attend a meeting. When I arrive, I'm the only one in the office meeting room other than the VP pulling the stunt.

I'm told by the marketing director to attend a video about one of our products. The video is an IUD-insertion training film, and only the VP and his male marketing assistant are there. They smirk and glance at me as we watch an intrauterine device being shoved up a woman's vagina.

Is murder ever legal?

The more eccentric among them introduces himself by kissing the back of my neck while I'm on a phone call, his giant bow-tie knocking the phone out of my hand.

These are scientists, doctors, and Stanford business school graduates, highly educated Mad Men. They believe themselves to be good catches, even the married ones. They expect their attentions to be received with humor and appreciated as flattering. Attractive enough to be nailed? Consider it an honor. They fancy themselves.

Despite the constant and dreadful turmoil it creates in the workplace, liaisons are understood to be a good deal, a chance to sample the good life, maybe swing a marriage or promotion. My boss tells me I better pick one of the available men and get married soon, reminding me that at my age "most of the good ones are already taken." The hunt is on. I am expected to enjoy it. This is the game of life.

I try to be civil and distant, familiar misunderstandings arise. I'm accosted by one VP who stops me in the foyer and demands to know "Why do you hate me?"

As seems to happen, he has the impression I play with everyone except for him. Trying not to be rude, I do my best to set him straight, to assure him I hate them all equally.

Although, I don't hate them. They are bright and interesting. Why would I not be delighted to have them attracted to me? What joys await! They are well-dressed, well-educated, and earning money. I think I should be flattered too, but I'm not, I'm terrified.

None of them realize their attentions make me vomit in the ladies' room. The pursuit leaves me out-of-body much of the day. I'm good at my job, but when I have to leave my desk, I stare at the floor to and from the errand, praying no one will intercept me on my business. Avoiding eye contact is the only way to be sure I send no miscues.

The internal thrum never relents. I spend off-hours holding onto Beau, wrapped in blankets in my closet. When I do sleep, sometimes I awaken to find myself standing and staring out a window or outside in the backyard, once out in the street. I wake myself up with the sound of my own yelling and find myself hurling about blankets and pillows.

I try. I let them nuzzle. I let them buy me champagne and take me to dinner. I let them drive me around in their hot cars. And I shake internally, throw up when I'm alone, and test the razor blade every night.

While I work here, running becomes the rage, and I envy my co-workers who take off after work with their long legs in their short shorts heading into the Palo Alto hills. I sign up at the YMCA for a beginner's running class. At first, I run 60 seconds and walk 90. Then I run 90 seconds and walk 30. In a few weeks, I can run the full 20 minutes, and then I run out the door.

I run forever. No one appreciates an endorphin rush more than I. From the Stanford telescope, I head off on the trails through ravines and brown fields, roaming the hills as I did when I was a little girl here. I run hours at a time and spend days feeling as if my feet don't touch the ground. I even begin to sleep through the night.

Feeling rested and strong, if socially retarded, I decide to take my boss's suggestion, and I apply to law school. I still want to change the world. I'm looking for a path, and being a student always seems like a good idea. My boss writes a great recommendation and I get into Santa Clara, my first choice. It's familiar territory and I won't have to relocate.

With a short time left before law school begins, company reorganization brings change. My attorney-boss-now-mentor departs, and I am re-assigned as administrative support to a Dr. Scientist. A few weeks in, he invites me to go with him to the city for a conference where he will be speaking. Then he asks if he can drive the Austin Healey. I have it on loan from my mother, and it sits parked in the lot.

Dr. S's hobby is driving race cars. I've heard he considers himself nearly a professional. Still, no, is the correct answer to this question, but he is my boss, and I would like to go to the conference.

I answer, "Yes, of course."

We travel straight to the city on Hwy. 101 for the drive there. On the way, Dr. S is quiet and intense, absorbed in revving, downshifting, and weaving through the heavy morning traffic. As the quiet extends, I assume he's also rehearsing his presentation.

Once we arrive, we mill about with other well-dressed participant strangers, sipping tea and coffee from Styrofoam cups. A steel-grey matron drifts in beside us. Dr. S turns and makes polite conversation. He introduces himself and mentions the paper he will be presenting. She refers to a specialized procedure being used at her hospital.

"Are you a nurse?" Dr. S inquires.

"No dear, I own the hospital." She hangs on the "o."

The chill hangs in the air. We drift away, stifling giggles.

After he gives his talk, Dr S suggests we return to Palo Alto via Hwy. 1 along the coast.

"Do you like calamari?" he asks.

'Yes," I lie. I have no idea what calamari is, but it sounds like something a worldly person would like. I aspire to worldly.

He knows a restaurant in Miramar that serves the greatest calamari. "Let's go!"

He's lighthearted, almost giddy. We hit Hwy. 1 and he plays race car driver on the sweeping curves, the Pacific Ocean cradling us on one side, gentle brown hills on the other.

We find the restaurant he's headed for and seat ourselves inside. The white-aproned waitress carries menus to our table, but Dr. S waves her away.

"Calamari, sweetheart. Pile 'me high."

I still have no clue.

While we wait, we chat, forced banter. He hasn't the quick humor of my previous boss, so there is nowhere to hide. Laughter makes awkward conversations so much easier.

He is a serious man doing serious work, and now he turns this seriousness to me. He wants to know who I am.

"Tell me everything." He rests his folded arms on the small round table and leans in, his eyes steady with sincere interest, although I suspect him of being sincerely interested in my being interested.

I make things up until the calamari arrives, then I'm punished for feigning sophistication.

The white apron delivers a plate piled high with tiny fried squid.

Dr. S comes close to clapping his hands in glee, purring his appreciation to our benefactor.

Calamari? Is this like renaming rockfish?

I hope my face remains neutral; my insides revolt.

I am expected to eat this and pretend to enjoy it?

They are leathery, tasteless, and upsetting. I don't admit my charade, but I can't swallow more than a bite.

Satisfied enough with my excuse that "I just am not very hungry," which is very true, he polishes off the plate of squid alone, and we return to the Healey for the drive back to the office.

Back on the highway, he downshifts and takes a corner a little too fast, working up to the real reason I've been invited along. Sailing around another curve on the narrow, two lane highway, he gets to it, "So…I know a great motel, just up here…"

The suggestion hangs. I don't hear the details. I'm disappointed; it's never just the pleasure of my company.

I decline in as kind a manner as I can muster given that he is my boss and driving my mother's car, currently at a rather high rate of speed.

As with the others, disappointment is not what he anticipates. If I understand the game, he expects me to be flattered, and to a degree I am, at least he doesn't believe he can just pull a gun on me.

He has worked himself into such a state that as I am mumbling what I hope doesn't sound like too much of an apology, he over-steers on a tight curve, does a 360-degree spin across both lanes and comes to a stop head-on with an approaching station wagon full of children and a terrified driver.

His race-track training kicks in, and he has us back in our own lane before we kill them or ourselves, but he's shaken. I was already shaken, so a near-miss, fatal accident doesn't rattle me much further.

In the ensuing weeks, before I leave to begin law school, we do a lot of pretending that neither the brush-off, nor the near-death experience, ever happened.

CHAPTER 12

Seeing the Wind Blow

I love the fact that I'm going back to school. The corporate world is too ravenous, too variable. I love the idea of returning to the familiar anonymity of academic routine, and despite what has become chronic discomfort around other people, I aspire to arguing before the Supreme Court—just one good, life-changing argument.

Before school begins, I decide to cut my long hair, care and morning prep taking too much time. I've heard that law school is frantic. I make an appointment at the I. Magnin salon in the Stanford Shopping Center.

Once seated for my appointment, I explain to the stylist that I need an easier routine. He begins at the back of my head and cuts my hair to barely an inch long. By the time I realize how short he's gone, it's too late. I'm nearly bald and I'm shocked, stunned. As I begin to react, the stylist repeats that I said I wanted it simple.

I sit in the chair staring at myself in the mirror, and relive hanging naked from the ceiling, pleading to strangers not to cut it. It's been seven years, but the memory cuts me open, tears spill over.

The stylist is offended by my reaction, naturally but wrongly assuming it to be a judgment of his work.

"Everyone should have to know how ugly they really are," he sniffs, as I leave the chair in tears. I don't disagree with the sentiment, but his timing is very bad.

Law school begins despite my drastic haircut, and despite promising myself I will give it my all, I get off to a weak start. After driving to the class orientation party, I can't make myself go inside. I sit in BMP, parked outside, and try to stop shaking, but cannot make myself open the car door to get out. I am too bare and I have nothing to say to anyone.

I return home and sit on my bed, bleak with disappointment in myself. I unwrap my razor blade, letting one thin, red line loose before setting it down.

I promise myself I'll do better once classes begin. I promise myself I'm going to be fine, really. I quickly break the promise.

A few days into the start of classes, I horrify myself by asking a fellow student to move to another seat so I can have the one she occupies. The seat is "mine," the one I've chosen in my need for routine, the one I have been aiming for, the one in just the right place.

When I first ask, the auditorium is empty except for the two of us. I have available to me at least two hundred empty seats. I try explaining that I need to sit in that exact seat, that none of the others will do, but I don't know what to say. I try making a joke of it, a deadly serious one, but it falls flat.

After I make the request, she frowns and stares at me. She doesn't speak; neither does she get up to move. She takes a drink from her coffee and continues staring.

I cannot believe I've just embarrassed myself like this.

Why do I have to sit here?

I'm as confused by the need as is she. I don't understand why, but I really do need to sit here. It is the seat I've been aiming for since I left my front door earlier that morning. This is where I am going. Now I am here. Now I sit down—in this seat.

No, I'm fine, really.

I am too frozen to say anything more. I stand as naked and stupid as I have ever been. We have a standoff. I burn with shame. Other students are taking seats around us.

I don't relent; I can't. Without speaking, she finally grabs her belongings and moves to another seat, staring at me in what appears to be both bewilderment and contempt. The embarrassment of this moment follows me for my remaining three years of law school. I never find a way to explain it to her.

For my first year of school, I'm awarded a scholarship and work-study. I work with San Mateo County Legal Aid drafting declarations for protective orders, meeting with nearly 400 women in the time I'm there, writing the stories that explain their need for legal help, in every case need for protection from an abusive man.

The women tell me of pain and fear, and more pain and more fear. My petitions for their protection are never refused. The community of hurt makes me feel less alone, but not better.

All of my classes in the first year of law school are yearlong courses, except Criminal Law. This is a one-semester course, at the end of which, exam results for this class will be a final grade. We'll have second exams—second chances—in the other classes, but not this one.

I enjoy law school and I work hard to understand the concepts behind our justice system. Free speech and the Fourth Amendment are particularly fascinating. At the close of the first semester, I settle in for my first law school final exam, the Criminal Law exam, with confidence. I test well.

The test has the standard three essay questions, three hours to complete them all. For the first question, the crime is rape. The girl, stranded, raped...

I get lost. I can't see. The sounds of the other test-takers get too loud, the scribbling of pens and shuffling of feet bombard me. I have to think. I can't write. I can't breathe. In moments, I'm flying around the room on the ceiling.

I flash through my own kidnapping, the dungeon, the long night. I try to focus. I have to focus. I have a scholarship; this grade is important.

I waste thirty minutes lost in my own nightmare.

When I regain a sense of where I am, I'm exhausted, and my full-body tremble makes writing nearly impossible. Whatever legal analysis I come up with is largely illegible.

I get a C, my first ever, but I'm relieved to not fail entirely. Despite my aspirations, a future in criminal justice slips away. It seemed possible until I discover I can't face the reality. To take on violence and injustice, I'd need to be able to stay conscious.

I interview for a job through the law school career office only once. My interviewer brags that she's the first female to be hired by her particular firm. The thought crosses my mind that this isn't much of a compliment, it just means she is no threat to the men, but her perception is otherwise.

After extolling her own success, she praises my academic record, then frowns and asks, "But what have you ever done?"

Although I have found it exhausting, she apparently does not find mere survival to be much of an accomplishment.

I have no response. I cannot explain to this stranger why I have no extracurricular or professional accomplishments. I cannot explain to anyone why I am lucky to make it to class and back home without breaking down, why I can't do anything but go straight home and hold onto Beau.

I don't tell her anything. Instead, I thank her and take my leave. No need for either of us to waste further time.

The world takes a turn at the end of my first year of law school. My high school friend, who continues to work at the company I left, lures me to a party hosted by former co-workers. I go in hopes that familiar faces will ease the loneliness of this school year, and I hit the jackpot.

I fall in love. I recognize the gentleman from his deep voice; we had spoken several times on the phone at work. He is smart, quiet, and handsome; shares an office with my GF and a birthday with me. We are Gemini twins, born the same day—I am four hours older than he.

My GF is sure we are a match. She encourages us to host a mutual twenty-eighth birthday party, and she turns out to be correct. He makes me laugh, and he makes me feel safe.

He invites me out, and on our first real date, a bar-fight breaks out behind us as we sit down for dinner. He excuses himself, gets up and grabs the offender by the scruff of the neck and escorts him outside, returning to the table and resuming our conversation where it left off. He's the coolest guy ever.

I maneuver the demons that haunt me, that are ever present, working hard to be alone with this good man, though as with Chinese food and Happy Hour, it's never quite as much fun as it might have been, should have been, but I succeed often enough to not drive him away, or to have to abandon him myself.

Distracted by romance, I spend less time figuring out how to save the world and instead hide away from it with him. He seems to understand that I need protection, and he provides it.

Beau loves him too, and we soon form a new family.

In June, 1981, I turn thirty, marry, and graduate from law school. My class standing isn't high enough to impress anyone, but I do okay. I survive.

So, that's what I did, bitch.

We marry in a church in downtown Palo Alto familiar to us both from our childhoods. I walk myself down the aisle, stumbling once into the chairs, my legs shaking too hard to be fully functional. I wish then that I had chosen to wear flats rather than high heels, or that I had someone to walk with me, but as I right myself from the clattering chairs and straighten my veil, the guests' laughter at my faux pas fading, I can't think of anyone who might have played the role and given me away. I would have asked my mother's husband, but her marriage has by now dissolved, blending never went well. Their acrimonious divorce assures that I'll see neither my once-stepfather, nor step-siblings, again.

My new husband and I move to a small cabin on Skyline Boulevard. The cabin rests on a sunny rise surrounded by fir, redwoods, and fields of lupine. Across the quiet, two-lane highway, forested mountains stretch to the ocean. Chipmunks, quail, and hawks patrol the yard and sky. Barn owls hoot their secrets to one another in the deep night.

I take the bar exam and while I wait for results and the summer wears on, I hike with Beau in the forest. We startle deer and quail, one day disturbing a bobcat. When the huge cat appears on the rise, Beau looks to me for assurance that he isn't expected to chase it. When we look back, the cat is gone. We're both relieved.

My husband's co-workers become my friends too. We throw parties; they invite us to theirs. We hike together in the forest and abandoned apple orchards. The wives and girlfriends take me in. We attend their weddings and hold their newborns. I become part of a larger world.

But I remain dark, never truly embracing friendship from the other women. I watch them enjoying one another's lives, but I don't share their warmth. I feel awkward and distant as if I'm hiding something important or am only pretending to feel welcome.

Their company makes me lonelier, it being so obvious they have something I'm missing, or perhaps the reverse. To me, it looks like happiness, a lighthearted freedom. I can find no excuse for not sharing it, but I don't.

I lie awake at night beside my husband utterly confused. I'm loved and safe. I even have a large family now—his extends around me too. Family events re-create Norman Rockwell paintings. I am welcome, but attend the gatherings feeling empty and sad.

One warm afternoon, Beau and I emerge from our hike in the forest and pause at the edge of the two-lane highway, checking for unlikely traffic. A short distance away, two well-dressed young men are standing at the edge of the road beside a parked car. When they see us, they begin waving their arms and running towards us, shouting as they run. I don't recognize the language, but the repetitive call has the tone of a critical need unmet.

I panic. I know in my head that they are lost or that their car has broken down, that they need my help, but I can't risk it. I run too.

I scream at Beau to follow me and we bolt back into the forest, leaping over logs and crashing through underbrush, determined to lose them if they are stupid enough to follow me in here. I slash and push and shove in a blind dash for survival. The void I run in is so deep, I die. I'm already dead.

I hide with Beau, burrowed in a decaying tree trunk. Terror takes everything out of me. I want to dissolve into the earth. I want never to come out. We stay until the night threatens to strand me in the dark, and I find I'm even more afraid of that. Apparently, whatever courage I once had, I've used up. Rational thought eludes me too.

Beau and I eventually wend our way out. The men and the car are gone. I hope another, more gracious stranger came to their aid quickly. I'm afraid to imagine what they thought of me, or what they knew I thought of them.

I still dissolve into tears when I'm alone and at random moments. I'm swallowed by sudden bursts of despair that leave me and everyone in my vicinity embarrassed and paralyzed. I have to switch grocery stores more than once, and I'm furious with myself; what more could a woman want?

I pass the bar exam and go to work as a family law attorney in San Jose. Work as a divorce lawyer is disturbing on all levels, the worst perhaps being the discovery that I am not saving the world—I'm big business.

My fantasies about an appearance before the Supreme Court quickly dim, and with my first pregnancy, I'm relieved to leave the work behind.

I love being pregnant. I feel legitimate. I can't be expected to have too much adventure. Staying inside and letting the world pass me by is entirely acceptable. I embrace it and am amazed at my own reaction. As with running, though I no longer do the miles, hormones take me with them.

We move from the cabin down the hill to Portola Valley. Soon after our arrival, I'm told that all the women here have Ph.D.s, or think they do. Growing huge with child, I lie in our sunny backyard and ignore them.

My first child is born at Stanford Hospital. Birthing itself, though arduous, goes fine, but moments after delivery, I hemorrhage.

I lie exhausted but thrilled on the birthing table and see the nurses' tensions rise from good to OMG. This is unexpected, and my Ob/Gyn—whom I can see straight-on through my knees—appears to be horrified. He also seems to be trapped, holding my insides in.

He calls urgently for plasma. Nurses scurry around the room, more arrive.

I don't know what the problem is, but I begin to have trouble breathing. I can't catch my breath. As I struggle, I curse the nurses and my doctor for being so preoccupied with the plasma IV that they're letting me suffocate.

With rising desperation, I try shrieking, "Oxygen, you assholes! Fuck the plasma!" (basic biology and courtesy escaping me for the moment) but manage only a strangled whisper.

I recognize this moment, the in-between when desperation hovers at the edge of whatever will be next. I gasp uselessly as the room slips away, my shocked doctor's face receding into the dark. Just before I am nowhere to be found, I see a robed, golden man holding my right hand. I feel his warmth and soft touch. I recognize the presence from my last visit to this threshold. He smiles at me as I fade away.

When I come to, boards securing IV-tubes are strapped to both my arms. Apparently, I have lost my blood supply and am being refilled. My baby is ready to leave the hospital days before I'm able to stand up.

I remain weak and anemic for months afterward. The sense that I live far away from everyone else increases exponentially. I'm barely present as a physical self, more a stranger gripped in a black hole of despair surprised to be experiencing it in this body.

I am mother to a healthy baby girl, privileged to be able to stay at home with her if I choose. The extended family is delighted with her birth. I smile and try to be joyful too, but feel only dread. The life I'm living and the life I'm experiencing are so at odds; I can make no sense of it. I'm hopelessly sad and feel miserably guilty about it.

Soon after returning home from the hospital to begin my life as a mother, I stand outside in our dark backyard looking up into the night sky, tracking a satellite passing overhead. I have the distinct sensation that Mother Earth reaches up through the ground, up my legs, through my abdomen and to my chest to bind me to her. My responsibility overwhelms me. I am grateful, but terrified. In this dangerous world, how will I ever be able to protect my child?

Desperate for the strength to meet this responsibility, while too tired and forlorn to do much else, I seek faith. I see its benefit in others. I crave the solace it professes to afford, and I've had glimpses of an Other. I'm curious.

One of the few possessions, besides what I was wearing, that I saved from the van when we abandoned it in Utah, was the King James Bible I took from the motel the night before I was kidnapped. Since that night, I've harbored a nagging suspicion that the kidnapping may have been punishment for taking it.

I assume Bibles in motel rooms are for the benefit of all travelers. I can imagine no worse sin than stealing someone else's chance at redemption. When I took the Bible for my own, I may have done just that. It's a niggling worry. What true faith I have is in karma.

And any explanation for my kidnapping sounds better to me than sheer randomness. I find this explanation plausible enough in a vast, incomprehensible universe. The idea holds both terror and solace.

My religious background is muddled. As a young girl, when I expressed interest in the church, my mother gave me a collection of treatises on the world's main religions and wished me luck. Later, I realized her faith was mostly Anti-Catholic.

At this stage, I lack belief but would settle for faith. I'd like to feel certain that someone is in charge, that we could improve things, if we just understood the tradeoff. I have a few questions I'd like to ask God. Nihilism threatens to ruin the rest of my life.

I decide to sort things out by studying this reminder of that miserable night, this reminder of what I fear may have been cosmic wrath. Taking my baby, Beau, and the Bible out into the backyard, I spread a blanket on the lawn and settle in the morning sunshine planning to begin again with the Gospels. My infant daughter lies on the blanket beside me gurgling happily. Beau stretches out for a nap.

Once my baby is content, engaged in rattle-mouthing, I thumb through the Book to the Gospels, laying it open to St. Matthew.

I smooth the page and begin the book of the generations, "…the son of David, the son of Abraham…" As I begin reading the small type, "Isaac…Jacob…" the world vanishes. I go blind. I cannot read who Jacob or anyone else begat. The Book, the pages, the names are gone. I see darkness.

Fear hits first, then the realization that my nightmare is real: I'm damned. I wish I knew why, though in truth I'm afraid to know, and just now, it isn't my highest concern. What matters this moment is that

I am totally blind and alone outside with my baby. Whether I have been thrown back by light or pulled in by dark, I won't ever know.

The blindness lasts long enough for me to beg. I hear my beautiful girl-child gurgling beside me, and I promise never to look for the light again. To whatever it is that plagues me, I vow never again to read the Bible or to look for God if I can have light enough to see at this moment.

My eyes clear and I sweep my daughter into my arms and run inside, huddling with her in shame. I don't believe in tangible Evil. I know this must be hysterical blindness, but I also know I dove deep and that I'm lost. Not having faith isn't the same as not being afraid of the dark.

I sink fast. Sleep deprivation brings waking nightmares. I try starving myself to death, but it takes too long. I know I can't die by my own hand. It will be too shameful, but dying is all I think about.

HIV is discovered to have contaminated a portion of the hospital's blood supply near the time of my transfusion. All of us who received potentially contaminated blood are called to be tested. I'm disappointed when the test is negative; I had hoped this would be my respectable way out. Otherwise, who knows how much shame I'm going to cause? How much more shame I will cause.

Barely able to move or communicate, I sit in the house, cowering in the wooden rocking chair, suspecting others loathe me as much as I loathe myself. I cry so hard I shrink to nothing, suspicious and inconsolable.

I'm delivered to another psychiatrist.

Dr. V is a large bear, tufts of grey hair sprout from his ears. I recite my life story. He declares a case of post-partum depression. I do little but cry in his office. I want to die. I have to, but I don't want to be disreputable.

I stick with it this time, doing my best to appreciate his professional services—no doubt he means well. He assures me no deity has an interest in my particular fate. I don't know whether this makes things better or worse, but he seems certain.

We try a variety of anti-depressants. Some create new realities, some paralyze. Finally, my difficulty undeniably existential, he sends me home with a copy of *A Course in Miracles*.

Support and good intentions go a long way, but I remain emotionally rabid.

In the *Palo Alto Times*, I see a therapist's ad for her study of rape survivors. I call, hoping she might find something useful in my useless self.

We meet in her South Palo Alto home. A grad student, she is petite and quick. In her gaze, I feel like a bug under a microscope.

She asks me to tell my story. I blah blah again. The tale is remote. I've told it often by this time. It hasn't much to do with me anymore.

Ms. Grad Student is rapt. I am rich fodder. She invites me to join her survivor group. I hadn't wanted to do this. More than one person in a room with me at a time is problematic—one is frequently too many—but she is earnest, and I want to feel normal. I want to feel like everyone else. I want to want something more than merely to survive each day without a life-threatening incident. I join.

With my fellow rape-insiders, I learn of many ways a woman's life goes wrong: friends, strangers, city streets, country lanes. I appreciate the compassion and strength of the other women. I add their nightmares to my own. It turns out we all feel alone, especially when we're with other people.

I make a friend in the group. We meet at Peets on University Avenue and reassure one another that we are still human.

She is the first person I've met whom I can talk to easily, who begins in the same place, a dark place we both hope we will one day rise from. And both of us fight the ugly wish that we not wake up in the morning. She also is a mother who doesn't want to leave her child behind, but who can't imagine staying alive either. She has trouble finding work and moves away. With this fragile connection to others severed, I quit the survivor group too.

The sadness and moody outbreaks don't relent, but I keep up with immediate demands. I try helping out at a day-care center and return home exhausted, less from the children than from working with the adults. I drop the ball and give it up.

Soon after, at age sixteen, beautiful Beau passes away. My daughter learned to stand by holding onto him, her tiny fingers gripping his thick black fur. At his passing, I feel his soul lift from my chest and drift away. The grief brings tears for many years. No other love is ever quite the same. BMP also is retired, overdue, and with the old car gone I feel a breaking of my last tie to much of my past.

As our first child turns four, I bear a son, complication-free, and as a family, we relocate to live in urban forest in the Pacific Northwest.

Our marriage survives a little longer, but after twelve years, we finally must divorce. By the time we give up, I'm a black hole. I know he loves me, but love struggles to survive in the best of circumstances; it hasn't a chance with such chronic, dark despair. He would have saved me if he could. The loss leaves me in shreds.

CHAPTER 13

Seek Knowledge, See Clearly

The children and I move a little farther into the forest. Our new home rests at the end of a narrow dirt road, surrounded by towering red cedars and Douglas firs. A small barn and corral nestle at the edge of a broad lawn. It's wild and still.

I am a lunatic. Anguish leaves me choking on my own heart, grief alternating uncontrollably with fury.

In my rage, I terrify my children, ripping through the house, shrieking demands, repeatedly threatening to kill myself or them. I scream at my small children that they should be dead, that we all should be dead, although I'm the only one who really should be. We are all, nearly always, in tears.

This leaves me with no choice. I have to die. Now, not only am I a useless coward, I'm a child abuser, a monster. But I can't leave the children behind. Who will love them as much as I do? I can't leave them. They are too precious. To protect them, I'll have to kill them too.

I know I must, but I can't do it. I don't know where to turn, the days passing in cruel confusion. How do I kill my children? Or worse, how do I die, and leave them behind?

Why didn't you just kill me, you fucking cowards?

Despite my desperation, my willing the earth to swallow me and get it over with, the damn sun keeps rising, and in desperation to find help, I do what I am most comfortable doing: I sign up for a class.

"Displaced Homemakers" meets once a week at the local college. New divorcees, and a few others lost as a result of cruel vagaries, learn to cope. We share stories and take aptitude tests. This time, army officer isn't on the list, foreign language teacher is my top career match.

I lift a little, realizing my despair, disappointment and sense of failure are so common, so typical. Except for the child abuse bit, I am fine, really.

However, once we get to the real-life exercises, such as looking for work, I drop out. I cannot imagine assembling too-nice-to-kill and going into the workplace. I have trouble navigating more than one brief errand a day before needing to retreat to the safety of my home. Holding a job seems unfathomable, though inevitable.

I have no credible, professional façade to present to potential employers, but with the class, I regain some control of my fury. Before I quit, we practice meditation, and I take the exercises home. They remind me of the before-times, high school and Waikiki, when my friends and I would gather for yoga classes on the beach and to watch the sun rise, pretending we understood cosmic mysteries.

As the summer wears on, I find a sacred place in the yard, cedars encircled by stones with three large rocks standing upright inside the circle. In the late evening, at the end of the day with the children asleep, I go outside and sit in the circle.

I take my shoes off before going in, and settle, folding my legs as near a lotus as I can manage. I light a candle set on one of the large stones. My mantra is simple. I let the clouds of thought drift by. Night closes around me. I slow my breath, inhale, exhale, until the kinks relax and the calm begins to feel real.

I sit in hope of finding answers. I want help, direction. I want to know why I'm never happy. Why I'm always sad or angry, sick to my stomach with fear, and irrational with my children. My patience with myself is exhausted.

This night, fury wells up. No more letting the thoughts just drift by, I hurl a demand at the Universe as I sit cross-legged, eyes-closed, under the cedars.

"What is going on here?!! Is anything going on here?!! I shriek in furious silence.

I hold my pose and demand again.

"Hello, Infinite, are you out there? What is going on here?!!"

I'm adamant.

I open my eyes and let out a sigh. I'm so stupid, so desperate, so very un-Zen.

The forest around me is dark and silent. I look out into the night. From across the broad lawn, near the corral at the edge of the trees, a small bright shape hovers at the fence line, then grows brighter or bigger, as it seems to approach my meditation circle. In a breath, the distance between us vanishes and the bright shape rises before me, stretching into the night sky. Magnificent, towering over me, it is the Thunderbird.

The Being stands before me, dwarfing me, radiant, wings spread above. His head turned in profile, one black eye above his proud enormous beak peers down at me.

My heart stops. I can't be seeing this—the Father of Healers is standing before me, looking right at me. The figure too grand to exist, the sheer scale too much. It isn't right. I'm so tiny, and...I just can't be seeing it.

The figure remains motionless, at least for the fraction of a moment before I slam my eyes shut. As I do, this grand Healer offers two instructions, four words, timely, succinct. I receive them, but I'm not certain I've actually heard anything. With the instructions ringing through me, I take a breath and peek, opening one eye just a little, both hopeful and afraid that the grand eagle will still be poised there, but It is not, the vision is gone, although the Being's stylized profile is embedded now in the stone in front of me, flickering in the candlelight. I can't explain it.

I go indoors to consider what just happened. I've had a visitation or hallucination—I hope visitation—and a good example of being careful what to wish for.

After checking on the children, I go to bed and let the night bring its own explanations.

It brings no explanation but the visitations continue. First, I wake in darkness a few hours later to an illuminated flying carpet hovering over my bed. Lights rim the edges and it flutters over me until it rises up out of sight, beyond the ceiling, disappearing far above me.

I get up and look out the window, but all is still in the forest outside. I slide back under the covers.

Then, two travelers pass through my room, walking at a slant to my reality and somewhat above it. One appears to be a trapper, the other Native American. Both are dressed in leather hides, metal bowls and sheathed knives hang from belts around their waists. They are engrossed in quiet conversation as they trudge on a forested trail that seems to run from somewhere else, through my room, and on to another place. I sit upright in bed. They pay me no mind.

Soon afterwards two fire trucks, lights flashing, arrive at the end of my dead-end lane. No one gets out. Instead, they negotiate turnarounds on the narrow dirt road and race back. They seem to be lost or perhaps practicing in the middle of the night. None of it is ever made clear.

Oddly, my encounter with the Great Weirdness gives me hope. I may be insane, but something is definitely going on. Who knows what, but definitely *something.*

I still cry too often. Leaving the house is difficult, and I rattle easily, but I know I can't kill the children, so I resolve to live until they can care for themselves and can understand why I could not live on. I try to follow the Great Healer's instructions.

Using the phonebook and trusting my finger to find a therapist, I look for a psychologist this time, as an alternative to my disappointing work with medical professionals, psychiatrists.

My finger lands on AC. He's a former Vietnam vet and within a visit or two, I'm pretty sure he's crazier than I am, but he understands. I find help for myself and my children.

We pace the park outside his office while he chain-smokes and encourages me to get mad at the kidnappers. My anger includes so many players by now that I only want to let them be. Let them all live their miserable lives; just make them disappear from mine.

We pretend, and I imagine grabbing the gun and turning it on them. I can't go much further. At that point, I would just back out of the room and go home, not quite what AC is looking for.

He hopes I'll act out my fantasy revenge but I can't. I don't know where to start, and I'm afraid to rub the hurt too much. I'm afraid I'll never stop, once I start acting out the real anger. I'm afraid I may be the most dangerous person I've ever met.

Revenge scenarios disappoint, but AC saves my children's lives. I stop raging at them, if not the occasional random stranger, and we work on healing family dynamics.

I still want only to escape life itself, and I know my children will be better off without me, but AC gives me enough strength to commit to mothering until I'm certain my children will be okay on their own. Once they're safe, I'll find a way to explain to them why I had to die. I begin writing my goodbye note, in preparation, but the efforts come up empty.

As we talk, the fact that I know so little of what happened after I left Utah, becomes a sticking point. AC offers to help me contact the Tooele sheriff to learn a little more about the aftermath.

The thought of contacting any of the players makes my gorge rise and my skin crawl. I don't want them to exist, let alone to interact with them. To them, I'm worthless. To me, they are. But my failure to follow-up on the details of my own life weighs on me. I'm guilty for letting them get away with it, for not stopping them when I had the chance. If I'd been brave enough to look, I knew enough to have found them, but I was not. I haven't been brave since that night and bear guilt for what the men did next.

AC gives me a chance to confront a little of this failure; he lets me pretend to be brave. From his office, we place a call to the Tooele sheriff. AC puts the call on speaker and explains why he's calling, "Might anyone be able to help us?"

We're on hold a long time. Finally, an officer takes the line and identifies himself. He assures us there is nothing to this story and thanks us for calling, adding "If ya'll ever get out here, we'll do some fishing."

AC and I are acting out the phone call as the voice lies. Both of us try not to laugh out loud as he repeats verbatim what was said to the Atherton sheriff in the first phone call twenty years ago, including the invitation to go fishing. The call works, anger overcomes humiliation, and I decide to look further into the details of my own life.

I visit my local library and read through old Utah newspapers, scrolling through rolls of film, finding nothing: no mention of any assaults, mine or any other, at this time, in this place.

I telephone the Tooele County Library and ask if anyone can help me find information about the events of that summer. An elderly librarian, who has worked in this library since before that time, assures me nothing like that ever happened in her community.

However, despite her confidence while speaking to me on the telephone, a few weeks later I receive a letter from her. In it, she has hand-copied a news article dated three weeks after the kidnapping in which Sheriff C calls me a liar.

Explaining that I had recounted an elaborate story and they were "still checking a few angles," he "seriously doubt(s) that the incident ever happened," continuing by noting I "gave descriptions that fit a lot of people and nobody."

Not as I recall it.

Concluding by dismissing me as a disgruntled hippie, he assures readers that nearly one hundred-fifty hippies pass through the county every day and that they've never had any trouble with them.

I write a note thanking her for her effort, letting her know I recognize how difficult it must have been to send the insult to me.

At the time, my local press carried an article in which the Utah attorney general assured our sheriff that a massive manhunt was underway. As nothing came of it, I always wondered about his sincerity.

I decide to try calling the AG's office to inquire. How much more insulting can they be?

No one has a clue as to what I might be referring to—a crime so old? Who cares?—but after making a sufficient pest of myself, I'm referred to the woman currently chairing a Victims' Rights Committee. She expresses concern and listens to the tale, now truncated to a respectable pitch for an X-rated movie, and promises to look into it.

Ms. VRC soon calls back, having found a court transcript of the unsuccessful prosecution in the case of the younger girl, the runaway I was told of while working for Ma Bell. She goes on to tell me that the two men were acquitted, but everyone in the area knows they were guilty, so they haven't led a good life. One may be in jail for pedophilia. I don't know which of the two men it is, and no mention is made of any others, but I appreciate her effort and hope someday it will make me feel better.

She offers to fax a copy of the court transcript to me. I can't imagine reading it, but accept the offer and thank her for her time.

Faxes are new and exotic. I drive downtown and pay a small fortune at the copy center for the pile I'm handed. The transaction is unbearable; my arms refusing to reach forward to take hold of the stack of paper. I burn with shame knowing this second attack was my fault and with fury knowing they got away with it again. As the clerk hands them to me, I wad the papers up and fight the urge to hurl them to the floor. Tears and nausea crumple me.

The confused clerk wavers between ignoring my meltdown and trying to help. I drive home blind and bury the pile of papers deep, not reading them. They never called me to corroborate or to identify, to help in any way. It is twenty years later. What could matter now?

My trail seems ended unless I choose to revisit the state, and I do not. However, the world turns again.

Not long afterwards, I receive a call from a Salt Lake City detective. Quite randomly, Ms. VRC found herself seated next to this officer at a professional event. She mentioned to him my rather bizarre story.

It is not bizarre to him. The details of the twenty-year-old crime she describes set off an alarm. He has in his files a cold-case murder from that time and place.

Detective T asks her for my contact number and calls me in my forest. His voice is quiet and professional. He handles me, not intrusive, not distant, but careful. I'm familiar with the technique by now.

He asks to hear the story, whatever I can tell him to help him with an unsolved case, revealing no shock as I recount to him a somewhat more lurid version of what happened to me. He is appropriately kind.

I give him what I can. I contact the Atherton sheriff's office, and they graciously dig up copies of my twenty-year-old statement. I haven't seen or read what I dictated to the officer since the day he wrote it out. I'm surprised by all the detail I included.

When Detective T receives my documents, he calls to thank me. He promises to stay in touch and reiterates that the Statute of Limitations has run for rape, but murder charges have no limit. I know this. I appreciate his manner. I have no hopes to be dashed, though I would like to help lay someone else's nightmares to rest.

He understands, or hears, the burden of my own guilt. He promises me the murder was not my fault, none of this, my fault. I want that to be true, but I should have pressed my own case harder. I know I'm a coward.

I can't stay on the phone any longer, saying goodbye and hanging up too quickly, grieving the death I might have stopped. I should have made them kill me.

Not many days later, Detective T calls again. He calls this time to tell me that he has investigated my story in connection with the murder.

He is convinced my rapists are the killers. They did not stop with me or the next girl or the next. Apparently, it wasn't until they had to kill that they gave it up. He notes again that the Statute of Limitations has run on all the rapes, and he isn't confident he has sufficient evidence to prosecute the murder. In his deep, quiet voice he lets me know the four men have gotten away with it.

He does want me to know though, that my story has been fully corroborated. Independently, someone else described the events of my kidnapping closely enough. There can be no mistake, it is official: I am not a liar. He wants me to know that everyone now knows I told the truth, that he's sorry about what happened. He thought I would like to know.

I am not sure why the sound of this stranger's sonorous voice relieving me of one particular humiliation overwhelms me, but this time the tears won't be choked away. I didn't realize I cared quite so much.

I thank him carefully, hoping he hears the truth of it as I struggle with the variety of reactions I'm having. I am grateful for his effort, his compassion, but it hurts.

His words rip something deep. I knew the men had gotten away with it. I have no disappointment to spare on this, but for the news that strangers no longer deem me a liar? It isn't relief or thanks that flush through me first, it's hate.

I could kill at this moment, something, anything. Lies are difficult things to overcome, but nothing compares to righteous indignation and mine is long-brewed. The night's cruel memories surge—the days afterward, the months, the years—why would I care now what they think of me? But I do. Wrapped up in fury and shame, I do care. It burns hot.

After the call, I sit outside in my sacred circle. I set a candle on the altar stone. The flame flickers in a chill breeze, its shadows dancing across the new Thunderbird etching. Darkness falls around me, beyond the circle.

I don't want the hurt, the memories, or the apology. I don't want to care about this. Once the burst of adrenaline subsides, I cry for a long time, trying not to care.

CHAPTER 14

As Yours With Me

The kidnapping must be laid to rest. No one will be punished for it, beyond perhaps a small degree of local, social ostracism. The first psychiatrist may have been premature but surely by now, I really should "get over it." Two healthy children, therapy, vindication, an otherworldly visitation—what excuse for my infernal sadness could I possibly have left?

The Thunderbird's instructions leave a lot to one's discretion, but I take them to mean that I have discovered enough truth to face life, to survive, and so, once again, as I'll not be leaving right away, I have to find a way to earn a living.

I resolve to go into the world strong, effective and happy, remembering always that I have a responsibility to my children and my pets, that I am lucky to be alive. I repeat this to myself at frequent and regular intervals as I head out, with every intention of succeeding, into the professional world. I am fine now, really.

I convince myself that I'd like to return to the courtroom, arguing in support of the distressed, maybe this time saving the world. Eloquent oration before the Supreme Court is still a favorite fantasy. I take and pass the bar exam in my new home state.

Seeking entryway into the legal community, to make connections, I volunteer with a feminist legal-aid center, assuming I will be less spooked in a primarily female workplace. I am mistaken. Immediately unsettled by the warm, all-inclusive atmosphere, too friendly even more difficult than unfriendly, I discover I'm not ready to be a co-worker, much less friends. The sheer compassion in the place makes me cry.

Everything about the job throws me: the technology I'm to use, the despair I hear from clients, even the drive downtown. My constant agitation destroys any confidence I have that I could survive a job interview, let alone convince anyone I'm capable of functioning in the fierce legal environment.

I look elsewhere. My foreign language skills being marginal, I consider the second highest scorer from the Displaced Homemaker career-placement tests: newspaper reporter. This idea appeals to me. I fancy myself uncovering secrets. Nancy Drew remains a literary hero.

My local paper accepts my services to cover civic meetings.

Before I set out to be an ace newspaper reporter, I'm under the impression I can do the job by attending, listening, writing it up, and sending it in—much the same misperception I took to law school.

Unfortunately for me, who cannot attend a public function without flashes of momentary insanity, reporters are not invisible or anonymous. It turns out they have to ask questions, introduce themselves to others, mingle in public with large groups of people, interact. I can't do it.

I manage a few printable stories, but soon give it up; far too many people involved. This career path, too, closes quickly.

Looking for more opportunity and less commute, after a year in the forest I move with my now elementary school-age children into the suburbs. As much as I want to hide in the woods, we are too isolated. The children need friends and I need employment.

In our new home, we have sidewalks, neighbors, and a community pool. I throw myself into the mothering role, volunteering in the classrooms, and joining the PTA where I smile and hope no one speaks to me, and prepare again to inch back into the work world.

Still unable to face interviews, despite being admitted to practice law in two states, I turn to temporary placement agencies to keep afloat. I don't have to explain myself to the interviewers. They've seen and heard it all and care only that I show up for my assignment, not why I'm choosing to work for pittance.

Working through a variety of temporary jobs, I cater, answer phones, and type correspondence, ashamed always that I'm not capable of working at the career level for which I trained. I spend nights in tears, huddled on the floor in a corner wondering, "What's the matter with me?" and I continue composing my still dreadfully inadequate suicide note for the children, just in case I am not as fine now as I'd hoped.

While rotating through entry-level clerical positions and trying to come to terms with my glaring inadequacies, I become obsessed with all things Hindu. I cannot explain it, but occasional obsessions are not unknown. I go with it.

As soon as we settle into our new house, I want to prepare and eat only curries. The menu drives my young son to plead one night at dinner, "Mom, could we please have some American food?"

I take to dressing in long tunics and pantaloons. In the dark of night, Shiva dances for me as I'm trying to sleep.

While this preoccupation is underway, our local paper carries notice of an upcoming visit by a Hindu holy woman. She will be performing a prayer ritual in a local retreat center. The address for the event is nearby. I drive around until I find it. It's in the forest, close behind the newer development where we now live.

The retreat's address post marks a long dirt road leading to a few wooden buildings. Once I find the sign, without thought as to why I've come, I turn down the road and park next to the first of the structures. As I do, a buxom woman with a swirl of long grey hair and a multitude of crystals hanging around her neck comes out onto the deck of the larger building and approaches my car. She asks if she can help me and identifies herself as the owner and retreat center's director.

"I live close by and wondered if you need any help with the prayer ceremony?" Until the words are out, I had no idea I was here to volunteer.

She does; they do. She asks if I can find flowers to be burned during the evening. I don't question the request, my lack of familiarity with Hindu ceremony total, but I offer to find some.

I set off through the town and into the countryside, passing aspiring wineries, stopping at nurseries and flower shops to ask for leftovers to be used in a Hindu ceremony. I'm surprised by the generous response. My car and trunk fill with slightly worn tulips, gerberas, and birds-of-paradise. Blues, purples, and yellows fan out across the backseat. I navigate the return drive peeking between irises, gladioli, and carnations.

The owner and her husband are delighted. They help empty the car. As they thank me and I turn to leave, promising to come back later that evening for the ceremony, the owner calls to me and asks if I need a job.

Just so happens I do.

She invites me in for a group interview which goes well. We hold hands and chant prayers. I'm hired as a sales director for the therapist training program she and her husband teach.

I love the retreat: the forest, the meditation room, the morning prayer and incense. My job is more telemarketer than sales director, but I appreciate the pretension, and I soon master the database though I'm never much of a saleswoman.

The center offers hypnotherapy training for licensed therapists and as a condition of my hire, I'm required to complete the program.

For a week, aspiring hypnotherapists and I meet downtown in a hotel convention center for lectures, and we practice the techniques in rooms upstairs. Participants from all over the country gather for training. The group reaffirms my perception that therapists are generally good, if somewhat disturbed, souls.

Towards the end of the hypnosis training, our aura photographs are taken. One by one, each hypnotist-in-training steps aboard the small platform facing the camera, grips the protruding handles, and awaits the flash. With the light, the handles give a minor electric shock and out pops a Polaroid photograph with our auras bright as halos around our heads. When it's my turn, I step up, repeating what I have seen those who precede me do—the flash, the tiny shock, the Polaroid.

Husband, who is handling aura photo-taking, watches my photo as it resolves in his hand. For those ahead of me, as it revealed itself, he and the photo's subject have exclaimed over the colors, the beauty, the truth exposed. However, as he watches mine, his expression goes from cheerful expectation to one you don't want to see on a doctor's face. He hands it quickly to his wife, head guru at the training.

She, too, shudders and shows me the photo. A blackened slash over the right side of my head interrupts the otherwise smooth mix of yellow, red, and orange blossoming around it. She steps away from me. In solemn tones, she tells me this indicates a Presence. I have an attached spirit clinging to me. I need an exorcism.

At this point in my life, I have been in the presence of an Other a few times. I know enough to know, I know nothing. I wonder if my Golden Man is actually a spirit hanging on my right shoulder, the way it feels sometimes, or if, as I suspect, I wasn't holding the handles tightly enough.

Husband will perform the deep hypnosis, not guru; she can't risk contamination should my rider be malevolent.

Skeptical, trusting if not convinced, I settle onto the hotel room bed, surrounded by husband, my co-workers, and interested observers from the training. I leave my shoes and sweater on, hoping being fully clothed will make this less awkward.

I've been hypnotized before. I cooperate and husband is proficient. Drifting away, backwards and smaller, never gone, I remain aware, but soon the goings on in the room don't concern me very much.

From my distance, I listen. Husband asks to speak to the Other One here. He cajoles and persuades. In my faraway spot, I'm a bit hungry, but decide not to interrupt the proceedings quite yet.

Someone speaks. A whispering male voice says its name. My throat feels as if I have physically collapsed, my windpipe resting on my spine. The whisper comes from me.

The voice names itself Ptolemy, going on to explain he's here because "he wanted to see, and she did not want to come..." I understand him to mean at my birth, (in which I took eight minutes to take my first breath, perhaps reconsidering, true), but the word he uses or the sound he utters, I don't understand. He may mean he hooked a ride at one of my other near-death experiences.

Husband tells Ptolemy he has to leave, "You're hurting her."

Where I'm resting while the two chat, I don't agree with this. I think he protects me—whatever he might be. Even if I'm just making him up right now, I like him. I've seen demons up close, this isn't one.

I think he's been with me a long time. Two memories remind me of him now. The second time, while heavily pregnant, I stood facing several angry men with chainsaws after challenging them for the destruction they were wreaking next door. I saw the front man look up, step back, and wave the others off. And for a moment, just a fraction, I was tall, really tall, and bigger. I startled him. I scared him. The men let me be, even as I called the sheriff on them.

And once before, when I was a young girl, an almost-boyfriend had the same reaction and I the same perspective. We never spoke of it, but for a moment, he was frightened of something we both were aware of, but that couldn't really have been.

The incidents stay with me, and as I hear this voice, I understand them, almost.

Ptolemy doesn't speak again. I wake up. Although I've been listening and discussing with myself the fact that I really am hungry but don't want to interfere, waking up is a bit unsettling. I have been gone, somewhere.

I open my eyes and sit up, looking about, quite rested.

Everyone in the room—it's packed—is speechless. Husband is gone. The therapists who were present begin recounting, first hesitantly, then stumbling over each other to describe what they saw and heard, as if I wasn't there. I was though. I heard it all. Hypnosis is odd.

My next aura photo is symmetrical, a blooming headdress with no black slash. The colors indicate I lack enlightenment, but no longer manifest a visual threat. I gripped both handles tight this time.

Neither husband nor guru wishes to discuss it further, but they don't fire me either. I keep the job.

The center hosts rituals from many traditions for their students. As staff, we may participate too, if we choose.

With help from local tribal members, we build a sweat lodge in the lush meadow behind the center, digging a fire pit, bending branches, and tying knots, then throwing blankets and skins, and more blankets and skins over the frame until the inside is dark and secure.

We inaugurate the lodge in early winter. A tribal ceremonial leader guides prayer and song, chanting and tossing sage and water on the heated stones with rhythmic precision.

Ensuring first that all attendees are accounted for—my job—I then join the others inside.

Night has fallen. I duck under the heavy doorway covering, still folded open; a light snowfall chases me in. Searching for a spot to sit down, I glimpse the others in the dim light seated on the grassy floor, a mélange of arms and legs packed closely together waiting for the ritual to begin.

I settle down onto the crowded ground and the final blanket is unfolded to cover the doorway, enveloping us in complete darkness.

I panic.

It is too dark, too crowded, too hot, and I am about to suffocate. I'm sure of it. First, I scrabble frantically at the wall coverings behind me, trying desperately to burrow underneath. Finding none that give, I leap up and come very close to falling into the fire pit, now hissing with lava stones, before the ceremony leader gets a grip on me, and holding me tight, whispers in my ear, "Be humble with Mother Earth."

Thank you, Indiana Jones.

I understand immediately and drop to my knees, burying my face in the cool ground. Breathing in the soft mist of the grassy earth beneath me, I let her hold me close.

The next few hours are my best since pre-birth. We cycle through prayer and song, the rhythmic chanting and hiss of water on fire, the suffocating heat made delicious by the fresh earth close to my face, Paradise.

Snow falls while we're inside the sweat lodge, sending our prayers to wherever they go. When we emerge from our cocoon into the chill night, I stumble, happily blind, into a wooden post and knock myself out.

I wake up awhile later in the snow with a bloody nose, alone in the dark on the ground. I wonder about the therapists who left me lying there, supposing I was not the only one transported by the evening.

I last a year as salesman. By then I have pitched the program to every licensed therapist in this country and to many in others, more than once. I can't do it anymore. Guru wishes to sit beside me, plugged-in to my sales calls, so she can teach me to psych therapists into buying her training. I'm reminded of work in the fifth-wheeler. I quit at the one-year mark.

Just before I resign, the Hindu holy woman and her entourage visit again. For a week, the center rings with ankle-bells and smells of sandalwood.

Her Holiness is frail, her smile guileless. For her time with us she remains aloof and none but her closest attendants come too near.

During the week, I participate in prayers and rituals in anticipation of the final night when I will be allowed a face-to-face with the Divine One.

This entire year I have been looking forward to being in her presence, to receiving her blessing. I'm grateful to have a second chance. After providing flowers for her visit the previous year, I didn't stay long enough at the ceremony to see her. I wasn't wearing all white as required, and though they gave me a white jacket, I was so obviously out-of-place that I couldn't overcome the self-conscious start, and once the djembes set up their beating and smoke from the burning flower blossoms offered in prayer on an open fire filled the room, I fled.

This time, I'm excited and comfortable. I am garbed in white, and I am among co-workers, not friends exactly, but at least familiar. However, when my turn comes I can't move. As she reaches me in line, I can't step forward. I don't want the crowd to look at me, and I can't meet the woman's eyes. Standing frozen, I stare at the floor wishing once more that I could die or disappear.

I miss my chance. There are many of us, time is short. She moves on to the next blessed soul. I stare at the floor and fight tears.

I don't know why I can't face her, why I can't let her see me. I don't know what it is that I'm afraid she'll see, or worse perhaps, what she will not. I don't know whether it's compassion or discernment I'm more afraid of. I'm ashamed to fear either.

And I may be afraid of what I might or might not see if I look at her, reputed to be the embodiment of love on earth. I need her to be the real deal, but don't give myself a chance to find out. I chose to leave her on her pedestal. The very idea of her must suffice.

CHAPTER 15

Vain Enough

Disappointed again by my self-consciousness, I carry the regret away as I leave the job.

Next, I go to work for a community college, providing clerical support for program directors. As much as any work does, the job suits me: I'm comfortable on a college campus, the work is detailed, does not involve the public, and it comes with health insurance.

With the insurance comes Prozac. My new doctor notes that I cry in her office when I visit and soon suggests it. "Just a small dose," she advises.

Dosage goes up quite a bit, but within a few months I feel better. I settle into the job; its details and quantity distracting and challenging. I begin to feel competent. My ego is rewarded when we move to a new building, and I'm given my own office with a door that closes.

I arrive for the first day in my new office with the door that closes, carrying a large, potted ficus. I work my way through the new hallways cheerfully greeting co-workers from behind the spreading foliage as I pass. Everyone is very grumpy. I assume we are collectively disappointed in the new place.

My boss greets me with a tragic tone, "Good morning."

Clearly idiomatic, not literal.

"Do we hate the new building?" I venture; her sobriety unsettling.

"You don't know." Shaking her head, she notes and informs simultaneously.

Taking my arm, she leads me to the break room. The TV is on, showing footage of airplanes flying into skyscrapers. I'm embarrassed that I live in such an isolated bubble. I didn't know. From here on, I turn the radio on first thing, just in case the world has ended while I slept.

While steadily employed and medicated on Prozac, I live a life more social than I would ever have believed possible. The children do well too, relaxing around me, bringing home friends, succeeding in school.

I no longer fear everyone on sight. I feel almost good around other people, sometimes. I get to know neighbors and parents of children's friends. One invites me to attend church.

Before leaving Portola Valley, two years after making a bargain with my darkness not to seek the light again, and after reassurance from Dr. V that it was indeed hysterical blindness, not an Almighty reprimand, I gave faith another try. An old church stood a few blocks from our home, and I sought there membership and baptism for myself and my children.

The minister welcomed me to the parish, and upon hearing of my writing experience, invited me to take over their newsletter production. Its two editors, he informed me, had been serving at the position for many years, and he was certain they would appreciate relief.

I attend the meeting wherein he announces to these women that I will replace them as newsletter editor. Apparently, he had neglected to mention this in advance to either of them. This is the first they've heard and they are insulted and furious. From this point on, when I enter the church for services, they and their families shift seats to avoid being seated too near me and mine.

Another church elder recounts scandal about a family who has just purchased an historic home in Menlo Park, then tells me if I repeat the story to anyone, she will call me a liar.

So far, I have been less-than-impressed with practicing Christians. The final blow comes when I attend a neighborhood tea and a brittle female across the room informs me that "this isn't really your neighborhood."

But the women at this congregation in my new home state are welcoming, and I need their friendship. I avoid stepping in to supplant anyone.

I attempt to embrace church ideology. Wanting to belong, I attend, participate, study. I celebrate my birthday away at a prayer weekend. The attendees give me flowers and sing "Happy Birthday." I have never had such a thing happen to me, to be a welcome member of anything is a surprise.

I host Bible study and set out teacups and cookies. As the weeks go on, I'm amazed by the women who gather, amazed that they come to my home, that I belong to this kind group, that I have found a place among them. But I rarely stay in the room during the entire study, too many people in it.

I'm invited to a monthly dinner with member neighbors, three couples and me. The first few evenings I enjoy the company, but once the newness wears off, I grow uncomfortable around them. The men pontificate, the women defer. I come to pity the second and to dismiss the first. I grow less welcome.

And after a little study, I can only pretend to embrace their faith, the overall patriarchy rather too self-serving. I'll be more inclined to believe divine inspiration when the one having it doesn't then put himself in charge. When the time comes that a man says he sees God, and God put a woman in charge, I'll be less skeptical.

As I pull away from the church, I abandon, too, the friends that came with it. It was mostly a package deal although I do the pushing away. I don't make a good friend.

After three years at the college, the longest I have stayed, or will ever stay, in one place, I convince myself I want to quit the job in order to open my own law practice. I'm drawn to the challenge, the role I might play in a grander scheme. I don't believe this job is the appropriate avenue, and the pay isn't enough to cover all the bills.

Given the road that led me there, I feel I was blessed to be given the opportunity to go to law school, and that I have an obligation to use the skills and knowledge I was given. I deem it my highest and best use, outside of my role as a mother. The conceit grows expansive enough to make leaving the college seem like a good idea.

I decide I'm foolish not to try. I'm admitted to practice law in two states. I have to take the chance. I still fantasize about arguing before the Supreme Court. But this time, I won't ask anyone else's permission. I won't try to explain myself. I won't be examined. As a licensed attorney, I can hang out a shingle and work for myself.

My decision to quit my job at the college is sped up by a meeting with the college president. I'm asked to attend the meeting by a union representative challenging a pay issue.

I am invited to never again attend a meeting, or for that matter to ever again be in the president's presence after vocalizing exception to a policy for employee salary overpayments.

The situation is patently unjust—the lowest wage employees being asked to repay an error made at the highest levels. They are entirely blameless. When she refers to the way this is "usually handled," I choke out, "This happens often enough to have a 'usual' way to handle it?"

The college president, who sits in front of me bedecked in enough gold jewelry to pay these employees' salaries for a year, uses her prerogative and asks me to leave; they'll finish these negotiations without me. As they should—I know nothing about employment law—but I know injustice when I step in it.

I take my sense of competence, frustration, and outrage, quit the job and open my own law office. I rent an office, buy books and sign contracts for ads and info access. I join, attend, read, hammer, and wire until I have an office ready to go. The shingle goes up. Attorney-at-Law, here I am.

Prozac works great.

Work goes well. I am soon swamped. My yellow pages ad draws in the wounded, and I set to work to save those I can.

However, having quit my job at the college, I lose my medical insurance coverage and the Prozac prescription ends. Despite the workload, my outgo far outstrips income, and I can't afford new insurance. I decide it's time to give the medication up anyway. I'm not at all worried; I'm fine, really.

Within months, I'm in tears from the moment I awake until I drift off for disturbed nights once again. My son wakes me calling down the hall, "Mom, you're yelling!"

I frequently awaken to find myself standing in the closet or at the window staring out at the night. My stomach hurts all the time. It gets difficult to stand upright. I wrap up a new Gillette razor and put it in my wallet.

Rage overwhelms me at the worst moments: in court, on the road, at random. In a parking lot, I leap to kill a man who has just slapped his child, realizing as I land in front of the man that he is enormous, and I won't make a dent. I slip instead to chatting him up about ducks and children and life while he stares at me, frozen, waiting for the attack he knows is coming, that he deserves, until his wife emerges from the restaurant behind us, and I step away, leaving him to explain the last few moments that include a welt on his young son's cheek and a blond, crazy woman.

On the road, I scream at and chase other drivers who I think threaten me first. I'm itching to fight, hoping and dreading, in equal measure. I embarrass my children, frighten and humiliate strangers, and wish I could die every waking moment.

I'm a danger to everyone, and I see no way out. I cling to the knowledge that I can die, just not quite yet; the children and our pets still need me. How could they possibly understand if I abandon them?

When not in tears or hammering out other people's legal difficulties, I work on my explanation, the note to my children that will explain why I couldn't cut it, why I fail at work, fail with friends, fail to deserve their respect. But the emptiness of the words makes it impossible to complete. No matter what I write, the words never capture it. My children deserve an honest, truthful answer. They love me. Before I slit these wrists, I better explain myself to them. This is not their fault. I can't leave it unexplained, but I can't explain it.

I keep writing, in hopes I'll have it completed in time, whenever that may be. I write on. We live on.

Despite being determined to succeed at the legal work, the abyss sucks at me. I stop taking new clients and fall behind in mortgage, credit cards, utilities. The collectors call. I'm sued for a debt I didn't know I had.

As the valid fear that I cannot earn a living melds with my somewhat-less real fear that the world is chasing me around, I try another doctor, this time a psychiatrist at my local clinic.

I explain that I had been on Prozac and felt good on it, so good I finally felt competent enough to open my own law practice. She interprets this to mean that I am manic and need sedating.

She prescribes a medication that encases me in cement. I become a sobbing bag of cement.

I throw away the drugs and don't return for a follow-up visit. I am only going through the motions. The medical profession hasn't been of much help to me, overall, and by now, I don't give a shit about feeling better. What would be the point?

By this time, I'm once again not able to trust myself in public. I explode with fury, hurling epithets and accusations at unlucky souls, or collapse into inconsolable weeping with little or no provocation and at the most awkward of times. Crumbling, haunted day and night by fears that make no sense, I give up delusions of a legal career. Having lasted one year in private practice, I close the doors and go home. My Supreme Court fantasy drifts out of reach.

I need income. I have children and pets to house and feed, overdue bills to pay. I pour over want-ads in desperation. Although I cannot imagine surviving an interview for a higher-end job, temporary positions won't cover the bills. I need real work at a salary above entry-level.

My resume is now bulky, if inexplicable. I concoct a story from pieces of my work history, find a common thread, leave off dates, and send it out, functional, not chronological. The lady who ultimately hires me says she called to interview me because the resume was so interesting. I appreciate the interpretation.

I'm hired after an all-day interview in which I sit in a conference room while prospective co-workers drift in and out, looking me over, some stopping for a moment to ask questions and then drifting on. I try to stay cheerful, to be someone they'll like, as I burn from the feel of their eyes on me.

I accept the job offer. The salary almost covers my bills, and after the interview, I swear I'll not survive another.

My new job takes me to regulatory affairs, my employers working to cure a dread disease. I'm hired to do complex document processing. The job is stressful and there are no private spaces. I sit in a line with other administrative assistants, facing a wall of company promotional literature and my computer screen, typing charts of numerical symbols and footnotes. My boss stands behind me watching me work, to make sure I get it right, and threatens to slap me if I touch her computer screen. As my mood darkens, she is frequently in danger for her own life but seems oblivious.

I'm swallowed by depression. My failures are complete, and I'm exhausted, always. During lunch hours, I walk around the block and sit in the local church. It has cathedral aspirations: elaborate gilding, statuary, candles.

I choose an empty pew near the front, not too close, not too far, exit within reach. I kneel and pray and cry, mostly kneel and cry. Even being touched by grace as I think I may have been, I have soul-strangling sadness.

This belief, that I received a blessing I've failed to fulfill or to honor, adds to my guilt. After such visions of a divine Other as I've had, I should be radiant. Why am I still a black hole? Why am I so useless? Why do I cry all the damn time?

Falling further into the pit, seeing nothing beyond my own death, I find a new therapist. She is slight and brittle. I cry and talk. She listens. I feel nothing from her or for her. I tell her I want to return to practicing law and don't know why I feel I can't. She assures me if I wanted to, I would. They think they can, because they can.

I tell her I want to die and ask if my children will be all right now that they are almost grown. She gets furious and berates me for even thinking about it.

"They will never recover!" She nearly shouts it at me, adding to my suspicion that therapists work very hard to heal their own hurts, in others.

I continue trying to compose a farewell to my children, but the note remains inadequate. Both children deserve so much better. I still can't explain to them or to myself why I would ever consider leaving them, but the desire to let this all be over is never out of mind.

So I stay alive but remain hopeless and out-of-place. I do only the minimum needed to survive. I cry while driving to and from work, at my desk, and at home. I try not to let the children see me dissolve. I lie to myself that they don't see or hear my despair.

My new employers don't succeed in their efforts to cure the scourge before funding runs out. As I hit the one-year mark, I arrive for work in the morning, open email to find I am summoned along with several others to a meeting, where we are laid off and told to go home.

Most of us are stunned. A few expected it or were insiders. I'm one of those stunned.

I return to my desk to gather the few personal things I've kept there. I disliked the job—the workspace, the tasks I did, my boss—but I needed the paycheck and the routine. I knew where I was going every day, and what I would do once there. Now I'll be lost again.

Shaking, tears slowly spilling over, I close down my computer; we're to leave right away. I assume they want us out while we're still impotent with shock. My fellow stunned admins and I exchange hurried hugs and wish one another luck before wandering out, all of us discouraged, angry and many, more than a little afraid.

As I drive home, tears give way to panic. I'll have nowhere to go tomorrow, no money coming in, no routine to rely on. The void faces me full on. The realization that I have to look for another job? Paralyzing.

I curse my stupidity. I should have seen the company's distress, should have been prepared. I should have known better than to trust doctors in suits.

School out for the day, the children are home when I pull in. They're surprised to see me. I'm surprised to be there. I explain that the company went under; trying to make it sound impersonal, not my fault, but I carry the weight of professional failure. It weighs a ton.

I had few expectations for parenthood, but I vowed to be a good role model. I wanted my children to find me admirable, to be someone they could look up to. I am not. I'm an embarrassment to them, and in front of them.

Setting down my belongings, I retreat to the kitchen. My son and the dog are playing catch. The ball hits a glass pitcher that I spent too much money on during a trip to Europe years ago, the last such trip I expect ever to take. Its slender neck shatters as it hits the cabinet on the way to the rug.

Seeing it broken, I lose all composure, howling in anguish, collapsing to the floor in tears.

My eldest is appalled. "It's just a vase," she pronounces, as one who is absolutely correct, though entirely mistaken.

I grab my purse and dash out of the house, afraid this time I really will kill her, or myself, or anyone capable of dying at that moment. I run to the car and roar out of the driveway, down the street and over the rise, pulling to the curb a block from the main road, coming to a stop beside the neighborhood marsh and turning off the engine.

Years of hurt, fury, and disappointment spill over. I pound the god-damned steering wheel trying to beat it into oblivion. Crying and cursing, I shriek at the universe for leaving me here without hope of shedding my nightmares or memory of the damned-rapist-assholes, and why can't I hold a job?????

I'm lost in hysteria, gasping through sobs, my head banging on the steering wheel, when a loud "Whap, whap, whap" hits the window at my left ear.

I freeze, then turn my head slowly to see the snug, black holster and tan-shirt belly of a highway patrolman standing beside my car. His motorcycle rests behind, angled to make attempted departure difficult.

Startled, I lift my tear-soaked, snot-covered face and stare up at him. His helmet visor is closed. His eyes large black ovals. I'm staring at a heavily-armed bug.

He taps on the window again and motions for me to roll the window down.

I shake my head. "I'm crying, not driving. Go away."

"Roll the window down, ma'am." His hand moves to his holster.

I have just about had it with law enforcement—there when you don't want them and nowhere to be found when you do.

I roll it down and let him have it. I babble, shriek, and sob, "What? I'm parked, legally parked! I'm crying. Haven't you ever seen a woman cry before? Don't you have a mother? A girlfriend? I'm not doing anything wrong! Mind your own business!! It's my car, go away!!!" All this delivered in an increasingly shrill roar.

"Leave me alone!!!" I shriek with my final breath, furiously rolling the window back up.

He doesn't. He demands to see my license, his hand now resting solidly on the pistol at his hip.

I am figuring a way to kill him first; this is my perfect opportunity. Can I rip his face off with my fingernails? Can I dig under that mask and blind him? I hope so.

"License and registration, please."

Deciding reluctantly against attempted murder of a law officer, I roll the window down just enough to hurl the two out. He picks them carefully off the ground, his huge, black-gloved fingers fumbling with the thin plastic license. Reading it over, he returns to his bike.

I wipe my face and pull myself together as best I can, exhausted, shaking from tears and now fear. I don't think I've committed a crime, but experience tells me that may not be relevant.

Suddenly, the sense that I'm trapped washes over me. Without thought, I open the door and leap out of the car.

"Get back in the car, ma'am. I want you to stay right there." His fingers tighten firmly around the pistol's grip.

I am not in the mood. I consider my options. I'm not getting back in the car, but besides slashing him with my razor, I'm at a disadvantage.

As we face off and I consider what next, a local sheriff's patrol car pulls up and parks in front of my car, effectively blocking me in. Apparently, the officers are busting me for crying in my car—hate and rage don't begin to cover it.

I swell. I leave the ground. As the two new pigs get out of their car and approach the HP pig, I slam my car door behind me and roar as loudly as I can "I'm going home. I have to make dinner for my family," shrieking this last to make my point.

Summoning the insouciance that has served me well in the past, shoulders back, reddened nose and mascara-streaked face high, I brush through the cluster of officers, ignoring them so completely that I cast a freezing chill as I sweep past, or I try to, at the very least.

I walk away from them. One step then the other, out back down, out back down. I head towards home, uphill, holding my breath, sort of hoping to be shot in the back—a totally legitimate way to go—but I hear nothing as the distance stretches behind me.

When I reach the top of the hill, the trembling easing, I realize my purse and keys are still in the car. I'll have to return, ruining my perfect exit.

I reluctantly turn around and see the motorcycle cop pulling away. He glances up the hill before spurring away around the corner. The local cops are already gone.

I return to my car and drive home. The children are mercifully occupied, and I face the reality of looking for work again, still a free, living woman.

CHAPTER 16

Carpet Ride

Job hunting has always unnerved me, but now the interview questions are nearly impossible to answer. I cannot explain my work history or respond to the implicit question when the interviewer remarks, "But, you could be a lawyer!"

No, I can't.

I can't be out in public or meet it. I can't serve on committees or drum up business. I can't stand before the bench without hating those on it. I can't dress for work without vomiting first.

Trust me on this, I can't be one.

But I won't say any of this in an interview. I'll smile and make things up as if I meant to do this: be a total loser scrabbling for the mortgage every month and having to leave carts of groceries at the checkout counter because I have "Insufficient funds." You explain it to my children, or better yet, go fuck yourself.

I don't know what the matter is either.

I count the days until I don't have to exist any longer. There can't be too many more of them, the time must be close. The date depends upon the lives still in my care, and finishing the note, so my children will understand.

The eldest will be safely away to college before too long. Once there, I never expect to hear from her again. Though she and I have healed some, she is wary around me, and for good reason. Telling her now that I love her doesn't make up for shrieking death threats at her in days past. When she again needs living quarters, she can stay with her dad. He isn't far away, but far enough to leave me behind if she chooses.

I need only remain living until the younger is safely away. I have to hold on just so long. The knowledge that I soon can safely slit my throat is helpful. I can find one more job. I have to. I'm fine again, really.

The firm laying us off offers a placement service package, perhaps in an effort to temper the rudeness of the layoff itself. I attend the workshops, respond to questionnaires, and cough up aspirations.

The final step in the career transition program is a meeting with the Big Guy himself, the man whose name is on the door. He will personally assess our accomplishments and dreams and set us on our way.

I'm nervous. Meetings with men in small rooms are torturous, but I show up. I wear my black suit and heels, and though no longer able to pull off model regalia, my lids too droopy for lashes, my cheekbones not what they were, I aim high.

I wait for my appointment in the spacious, fern-filled reception area. When it's my turn, I leave the other tense and hopeful former co-workers still waiting for theirs, to follow his secretary into The Office. My future awaits.

We've heard from all our handlers at this workshop about the great man's skills in developing this "tremendously successful" placement agency. We have been assured that we all have futures, and He will make sure we succeed in them. No pompoms or short skirts, but the message is clear.

All this will be available to us if we sign up for further assistance after today—this last bit added as an aside.

By the time I have completed this process, once again examining my own work history and uncovering a disappointing absence of any dreams or career ambition other than a general world-saving that hasn't shaped up as I might have hoped, I am hollow, well-dressed, but hollow.

I enter with all the aplomb I can muster and hope I'm smiling. Stepping forward, I try to appear grown up. I would like to have a career, perhaps a future. I am hoping this process will show me one.

Mr. Big is a large Suit, his office full of leather and foliage. I extend my hand as he offers me his. He invites me to sit.

I perch on the edge of an armchair cushion. Its proportions suggest it will swallow me if I scoot back.

My host remains standing, silent, seemingly perusing the resume he holds in his hands.

He clears his throat, "So…" His opening isn't encouraging.

He begins again, "So...I reviewed this resume and I've been excited to meet the person behind it..." He exhales slowly, "…and then you walked in."

His hushed tone makes clear this is not a compliment.

I have fully explored ways to disappear. I have willed it, demanded it, begged and bartered for it. It never happens.

Being told what a disappointment I am, after I have merely walked in the room, shames me beyond recovery. What presence I have mustered to this point, withers. I am taken back to my embarrassment with the TA at Cal. If he hopes I'll be inspired to greatness by his observation, I am not.

He goes on to contrast my experience with my lack of confidence—my presentation and demeanor are mentioned.

Once more, I can't hear very much beyond his less-than-helpful insight. I do wonder how much my former employer is paying him. I could have used the cash instead. I decline to sign a new contract for additional services, suspecting more con than compassion, and take my leave without thanking him. Tears don't fall before I'm outside.

Mr. Big confirms my fears: my nightmares are still smeared all over me. I'm a mess and everyone sees it. I should never be out in public. However, I vow that if one more male takes it upon himself to point it out, it will be the last observation he makes.

For work, I turn to temporary placement agencies again. Out of debt, the pets and I can almost survive on entry-level wages and with the temporary positions, I needn't feign self-confidence.

Over the next few years, I deliver junk mail, operate a printing press, wash dishes, answer phones, sort goods for United Way, manage a store, and maintain databases. I work as a hardware store cashier and neurosurgeon's secretary. Some of these jobs are meant to be temporary and some are meant to be permanent.

The reasons I leave the permanent jobs always make sense to me. The one thing they have in common is that I just have to leave. Before a year is up, and usually much sooner than that, I would rather die than do the job one more day, so I quit. I am a personnel department's nightmare.

One recruiter tries repeatedly to place me at Boeing. He's sure I will make someone a great secretary, but despite his enthusiasm, I fail the interviews. On our last phone call he suggests I use smaller words; it seems I'm intimidating my prospective employers. He hears a few select short words before I slam down the receiver.

Interspersed throughout these years, I receive calls about a job that I might fit. No mention is made of who exactly is hiring, but I am being considered for a vague "something" and they will call me back.

Someone else then eventually calls back, and we complete another phone interview. I chat with young men, older women, and then back to the young men. My story is consistent and almost true—I do want a good job. I'm a hard worker. My explanation for the inexplicable career path, not so much, but I stick to it, the demands of parenthood taking much of the blame.

Finally, I'm invited to a group interview and given an explanation: a formidable charitable organization is considering me for a number of support positions. They truly are trying to save the world, and I may be able to help.

At this point, I'm working three jobs: weekends, I'm a cashier; evenings, I clean a restaurant kitchen; weekdays, I process clinical-trial data. At home, the roof is leaking, and I'm struggling to make mortgage payments, to hold onto the house so my youngest will have his home at least until he leaves for college, only a few months away.

A job with benefits and purpose sounds too good to be true. I had no idea the series of interviews were connected, assuming they were random scouts. Hope springs.

For my first in-person interview, I drive into the city and once I've arrived at the gates of the nondescript building, follow the guard's directions to reserved parking. I'm shaking as I walk inside the entryway rotunda where I'm scrutinized by security, given a badge, and led to a spacious meeting room.

A variety of players introduce themselves, some well-manicured, some pointedly not. I explain myself a few times and I'm invited back for further interviews.

I return the following week for my next interview, still shaking, still dreaming of helping on a big scale. This time I'm led down hallways to various conference rooms where I chat with interesting, anonymous people doing interesting, not-so-anonymous work.

Approved for two openings, I repeat the process, coming back for a third round, after which the options are narrowed to one.

I arrive for what is to be the final interview, but only two of the three relevant team members show up. The third member asks that I return the following day.

The next morning I let my current temporary, weekday employer know I must once again leave work early. At lunch I go to the bank. When I present my withdrawal slip, the teller looks at me from under furrowed brows. She mutters to the teller beside her and a Suit strolls over, as does the security guard.

The sober-faced Suit explains there has been suspicious activity on this account, and they have to check my ID further. I then see the bank screen, and my account is empty. There was little money in it, but what was, is gone.

Proving easily that I'm me, suspicion shifts away and the Suit tells me debit numbers were stolen from a small business near my home. One arrest has been made—a young woman used my money to buy diapers at Wal-Mart.

The crime makes me sick on a number of levels. The Suit assures me my account will eventually be re-credited. I wonder what happens to the child who needed diapers. I return to work, shaken and sad.

To finish up my work day, before heading off to face the final hurdle for my dream job, my opportunity to truly be of help on a grand scale, I do the day's filing. Still uneasy and teary from my collision with despair and the banking industry, I shove a final folder into place and slam the drawer shut.

My index finger still rests on top of the files as the drawer clicks closed, latching with my finger jammed inside. The catch won't release until I shove the drawer in a little farther, finally unlocking and letting the finger go. The first knuckle is mashed, the nail dangling, slashed across the cuticle.

I have no time to spare on the wound; the job of a lifetime is nearly mine. My damaged pointer must wait. Wrapping tissues around the finger to stem the bleeding and to hold the nail in place, I gulp down four aspirin before heading off to embrace my future.

By the time I arrive, shock has worn off, but aspirin has not kicked in. The finger throbs like a bass drum, every beat wracking my entire body. Once parked, I really need to sit in the car and moan in agony, but I take a deep breath and get out anyway, going through security, cradling my arm and holding my breath lest whimpers leak through.

After seeing me to the now-familiar conference room, my escort opens a refrigerated drawer, offering me various beverages. I can only shake my head, afraid if I speak I'll burst into tears. I don't need Perrier, I need a doctor.

My potential boss slips in, his boyish face incongruous with his reputedly great wealth. He seems ill-at-ease, looking mostly at his own hands or perhaps his lap as we talk.

The interview proceeds in a blur. I'm frozen, a rictus-smile plastered across my face, the mangled knuckle and failing bandage clenched on my lap, its slightest motion stunning me. I assume he isn't noticing my occasional sharp intakes of breath, as he never actually looks at me.

The finger pounds so loudly I can't really hear him. I supply rehearsed answers to the questions I assume he asks. As the interminable moments tick by, I struggle to avoid holding up the throbbing digit and blurting out "I hurt my finger."

Apparently, he isn't paying attention either because they offer me the position.

I ignore the red flags: the dysfunctional team, the regimented setting, the nerve-wracking commute, and perhaps most obvious, my pre-interview self-sabotage, and I accept the job, entry-level admin, with a salary just barely enough to live on. For a very brief time, I cling to the illusion that I may have found a way to make a difference in the larger world.

The illusion evaporates quickly. I walk to and from work in tears and sit at my desk afraid to speak to anyone. I am so depressed by the time I'm hired, I will never know if I'm really ill-suited, or if my sadness is so embedded that not even the promise of world-changing innovation can lift me out of it.

I don't make it beyond my probationary period. I'm fired in person minutes after submitting my resignation to HR. In that at least, we were on the same page.

CHAPTER 17

Give and Take

With loss of this job, I lose hope of keeping my house, vital repairs and mortgage payments slipping beyond reach. But I've held on as long as I'd hoped to, my youngest child driving off to begin college a few weeks before I'm fired.

I watched him back his bright red Jeep, loaded to the roof with possessions making the right-of-passage cut, out of the driveway, and waved to him as he rounded the final corner, recognizing his huge grin as the smile of a young man on his way.

I want my children to fly. I want them to be adventurous and happy, but as my son drives off, I can't imagine the impending emptiness, the loss of the one remaining, loving person in my world. I can't imagine it, but it happens just the same.

I have longed for, and grieved this day, far in advance of its true arrival. I've imagined it empty of love or future. I know it as the day I can die without guilt. I've begged for it more than once, the day my role as mother and protector of these young lives is complete and I can escape.

But once the day arrives, I find I still am not the free bird I anticipated, the one who could easily slit her throat whenever she chooses. First, I want to watch my children grow on. I want that more desperately than I need delivery from what haunts me, and more immediately because I still have pets. I have seriously miscalculated my release date.

Over the years, I filled empty spaces and aching needs with family pets. First a puppy—she soon became Nanny and best friend, my young son saying she made us a family—then kittens, more puppies, reptiles, rodents, and birds. I assumed all would age and pass before this time had come, but they have not, not all.

Though both children are young adults and away on their next adventures, my immediate family still consists of a big dog, two cats, a lovebird, and a chinchilla. They are my responsibility. I owe them my protection. I can't, and in truth don't want to, leave them just yet. So I need another survival plan, another foxhole.

My job prospects are few. Being fired from this last position ruins my already ragged relationship with placement agencies in the area. I can explain my erratic work record with tales of family necessity, but not this failure. I've run out of excuses for my professional history, even entry-level work is difficult to find. Desperation and shame compete. I have pets to house and feed.

I'm saved this time by family. My mother needs help. Her home will accommodate my menagerie if I will relocate to care for her. Disabled and in unrelenting pain, she has exhausted other family members as caregivers, and although I am not her first choice, it is my turn.

My relationship with her remains awkward. I wish I had confided in her years ago, or she in me, so that we might have at least understood one another, but I suspect now she is beyond a time for reflection, and that I'll never know what truly troubles her. But she asks for my help, and I agree, hoping this effort might heal us both of wounds neither chooses to identify.

Before I can move to my mother's, or put my house on the market, which I'm desperate to do before I default on the mortgage, I must pack or discard my life's possessions.

I stand in my bedroom and consider the task ahead of me. The work must be done quickly, and I will be doing it by myself. I look around the room, drifting with the memories.

The good memories are so achingly wonderful and the bad so painful, instead of beginning to pack, I cry, my quiet sobs soon evolving to a mournful howl. I curse my weakness, my failure, the life that led me to this day, to the awful aloneness of this day.

I'm on the stairway in full meltdown when I see a young friend of my college-bound son downstairs, sitting at the computer. He's staring up at me, wide-eyed.

Except for the pets, I live alone. The house should be empty. Both of us momentarily frozen in place, he finally manages to stammer out, "(my son) told me it would be all right, even after he left..." His voice peters out.

It is okay, the friends have always been welcome, but I'm ashamed to be caught losing my mind in front of him.

He is painfully sorry to have intruded unannounced and offers his help. When it's time to empty the garage loft, once the boys' favorite hangout, I take him up on the offer. He and a few others of my son's friends climb up into the loft and hurl pillows, miscellaneous electronic equipment, and an alarming number of empty, red plastic cups out of the loft to the garage floor.

But first, when my immediate tantrum subsides (after apologizing and bidding farewell to the young man), I begin with my smallest dresser drawer, the one holding my glass treasures. I wrap each in tissue and carefully pack the fragile wads in a shoebox. It's a start.

It takes several days, but eventually I am hurling electronics and plastic cups from the loft in the garage. The home empties, decisions of which memories to keep and which to discard finally made. I give up most household possessions, assuming I won't need anything, my mother having what she needs, and I foresee no need of my own beyond the immediate.

The house sells quickly, just weeks before the real estate market crashes. I keep a small profit, enough to allow me to breathe for a time.

On my last night in this family home, where I raised my children and bid them farewell, I sit in the dark on a beach towel in my empty living room. My big dog Daisy and both elderly cats sit huddled beside me on the towel. They may not know what's next, but they know enough to stay close. I clutch my knees to my chest and rock slowly back and forth.

In spite of my constant fear and sadness, I yearned for this home to be the center of a joyful family life for generations to come. I dreamt of grandchildren, great-grandchildren doing homework at the dining room table. I fantasized about the children wanting the table or the dishware. I imply a longing for memories to them, but the longing is only mine.

It isn't going to happen. I give up this fantasy too.

At three A.M., I pack the cats and chinchilla in carriers, dismantle the birdcage, reassuring Sugar, the lovebird, that he will be fine, and pack them all in the back of my Honda station wagon for the drive to my mother's Nevada home. Daisy rides shotgun, and we head off in the pre-dawn dark for the eleven-hour drive to our new life. It all feels so wrong. I'm crippled with the pain in my gut, the hurt, the failure, the end that isn't yet an end.

For the first hours I drive blind, the highway a surreal blur of tears, rain, and headlights, but when dawn arrives, I am miles away and out of both tears and rain.

We head up into the mountains through deep forest and as the terrain becomes unfamiliar, the pain eases. I'm tired but alive and I've done it again, found a way to survive. Despite my worry that they would not, my children still speak to me, all the pets are safe, and my mother has asked for my help. Maybe I am fine, now.

The day wears on and a sense of adventure lightens my spirits. I haven't been on a road trip in a long time. Before the nightmare, I loved them. Daisy understands rest stops right away. She dashes, squats, and leaps back into the car with enthusiasm and good nature, an ideal travel companion. Sugar's call and response chirp still strong; the cats settled, both old and seasoned; the chinchilla inscrutable but quiet, we keep moving.

We leave behind forest, and the landscape harshens, sunlight glaring off the jagged mountain ridges. I have visions of opening up to the world, resolving once again to shake off my failures, my fears. I did not fail utterly as a mother, my only genuine commitment, both children doing well in the wider world. I might consider that a success. I'm certain that a new person, outgoing, friendly, and carefree, hovers just below the surface. I know I am truly a happy person. I know it. I'm fine, really.

When we arrive at my mother's home in the late afternoon, she is asleep and the house doors locked. Hard of hearing, she sleeps through my knocking on both the door and her bedroom window, my increasingly desperate pounding going entirely unheeded. After the eleven hour drive, I am somewhat desperate. But before I give up entirely—the pets can't stay confined long in the sweltering heat—she awakens and lets us in, seemingly surprised to see us, and leaving me wondering if she remembers we were expected, that she invited us. She remains curt and the stay begins badly.

The pets and I settle into a bedroom, all of us room well together though it is a bit close. The house is modest but has a yard with sun and fruit trees, and, despite the less than enthusiastic welcome, I commit to a happier life.

Daisy and I roam the bare hills, finding tiny islands of flowers in the parched earth. After the cloudy skies and thick vegetation of the Northwest, this open landscape and bright blue sky are breathtaking.

But my commitment to be in good spirits does not withstand the needs of my disabled, disparaging elder. She has been both disapproving and in great pain for many years, and is cruelly critical. The two combine to defeat me. I both understand and dislike her. Anguish eats me from the inside out. I find the harshest cruelty I've known so far to be that spoken in my mother's voice.

I spend a year with her. By the end of it, every morning I'm crawling from my bed to the bath at dawn to retch on an empty stomach. I lose thirty pounds before calling it quits. I can't make her happy. I can't make her love me any more than she will. I can't care for her.

Before I give up, I spend the profits from sale of my house on medical tests. I can barely stand any longer. The doctor rules out an ulcer, prescribes an anti-anxiety medication, and suggests Prilosec.

Instead, or rather in addition, I turn my mother over to caregivers better able to withstand her vitriol, and I move back to the Northwest. The pets and I survive the trip in reverse, as well.

CHAPTER 18

Fears We Live By

I settle into an apartment, not too near my old home, needing a chance to be someone new. I have no plan, other than to survive the pets, and to finish my explanation to the children for my suicide. I am still composing the perfect goodbye, perfecting the pathos so my children will forgive me for having terrorized them, for never being happy or successful, but the explanation still eludes me. I also keep the razor close, just in case things get entirely out of hand.

The anti-anxiety medication that the doctor prescribed just before I left Nevada makes the world around me clearer. With the calm it induces, I question my decision-making less, and the decision becomes firm: I have to die. I am a rational human being, reflective and certain I'm correct. I have no option except death.

I see the desolate path in front of me. The abyss yawns wide and dark. However, funds for medical care soon run out and when the prescription expires and the drug's effects wear off, this certainty wavers and then evaporates. Without the medically-induced sobriety, hopes and dreams begin again to intertwine with the despair. Knowing I can't be trusted, I have to once again consider all possibilities before making any decisions, meaning very few, if any, are made.

The returning uncertainty and its confusion allow room for the niggling idea that I might still be happy, might still be fine, really, if I could just understand what's wrong with me, just do something right. Manic or optimistic, I'm never sure which.

Hopeful or not—I'm volatile—I'm faced again with another job hunt. Rent comes due. Pets have needs. Having settled slightly south, I turn to a new batch of placement agencies, using "family demands" again to explain my sketchy work history.

I have recovered "too nice to kill" and, through the agencies, I work a series of odd jobs. I know I can keep it up for a while. The note to my children is coming along and the pets aging. I cling to the truth that this tunnel is not interminable.

A temporary employer asks that I stay on, making the job permanent. Accepting, I relocate within walking distance to the job. Before the year is out, the company suffers a set-back, and I am laid off.

For the few months I've been at the position, I have walked to and from it in tears, trying unsuccessfully to hide them while I'm in the office hallways and at my desk. I'm ashamed that I'm able to work only in such a menial capacity, an honest job, but menial. Still licensed to practice law in two states, I know I should be able to bear more responsibility. I wish I knew why I cannot.

Though the job was meager, and I unhappy, at least I knew where to go every morning, what I would be doing all day, and when I could go home. Without the direction, once again, I'm a black hole.

In the days following the lay-off, Daisy and I wander the pathways in the patch of urban forest around my new apartment and former employer, as I weigh my miserable options for beginning again. I cry. Daisy bounds.

One afternoon, an older gentleman also walking his dog on the grassy trail, comes across me crying and strikes up a conversation. He follows the path with me, recounting his experience as a military counselor, detailing his opinions about men who are depressed or "unable to get over it." We pause at a fork in the path, and I wait to see which way he's going to go, planning to head the other way. Instead, with the pause, he steps forward and leans in to kiss me.

I leap backward, sputtering in shocked embarrassment. He's startled that I'm not receptive, pointing out I'll feel better if I lighten up. "Lightening up" joins "Getting back on the horse" as strikingly self–serving euphemisms.

I'm far away down the path by the time he finishes his observation, and for a long time afterward, Daisy and I avoid going out.

After the stunned grief over this layoff subsides, and some relief to be finished with the job sets in, and after my encounter with another male whose solution to life's pain is to get laid, I get angry.

I become a danger once again to neighbors and strangers, finding reason to snark and insult anyone who gives me the slightest opportunity. Out walking, a husband moves to shield his wife from Daisy, and I chase the couple down the path, shrieking at their retreating backs that the only thing the wife has to fear is her husband.

I hurl myself into a man's chest and dare him to shoot me after hearing he threatened to shoot a dog. His children stand paralyzed as I goad and push, spewing hate and contempt at him. He calls 911 and I leave him on the phone describing the insane woman assaulting him. He's right to do it, but I wish he'd just shot me. These public rages are humiliating.

What am I doing?

I can't make myself apply for another job. I can't look anyone in the eye. I can't pretend I don't hate everyone for thinking they might judge me. *How dare they?*

As I perceive it, I'm faced with only one employment option, if I must survive, and I must—the pets still need me—I will have to open my own law practice once again. It's the only thing I can do that doesn't require begging someone else to let me do it, and I continue to grieve the waste of education and opportunity I've been provided. I would still like to succeed at being of help.

This time, I don't need brick and mortar. Times have changed, and I can work from home with legitimacy. I reacquaint myself with the head of a women's legal services group, and she sends me cases. Most are to be done for free, but I learn. However, from the first case, I'm turned inside out with nausea, once again sick with every dawn.

For a time, I pull myself together, and I succeed in straightening out child custody and support for a few whose lives did not proceed as planned. I handle several cases before I'm too weak to continue.

Another year has passed.

I realize I cannot function as a lawyer (or as anything else) and resign myself again to ending my own life. I have dragged it on far too long.

As I conclude my last cases, having decided that once the office is closed I will put the remaining pets to sleep and then follow them myself—screw the note—my sister needs a break from her role as our mother's primary caregiver. She asks me to relieve her for a week.

I don't want to. I'm physically weak and an emotional wreck. I cry all the time, and I can no longer stand up straight, always hunched to ease the ache in my center. And my mother couldn't possibly want me back.

Big Sis assures me Mom remembers nothing of my previous year with her and looks forward to my coming. I don't believe a word of it, but I know how difficult the job is; I can't truly refuse Big Sis.

I agree to go, and the chronic internal hum that plagues me rises. Agitation, low background fear, rides my shoulders. If my Golden Man is still with me, I hope he'll help.

The long drive to my mother's is physically and emotionally overwhelming. I can't face making it again. If I go, I have to fly, but I can't imagine navigating the hostile security scrutiny at the airport either. The very idea infuriates me: the lines, the stares, nowhere to look or to hide. I hate the prospect. But I commit to my family to help. I find care for Daisy and the cats and drive myself to the airport.

I'm afraid I'll get lost on the thruway to cheap parking, so I don't try to find it, paying instead for the easiest and most expensive parking. I have no nervous energy to spare. By the time I'm inside the airport, I am fully out of my mind.

I stand in the security line willing myself through it, silently begging them not to scrutinize me. I don't know what I am afraid they'll see, maybe just my disgust for the sham, but I hate to be looked at anyway, and I am wound tight.

I reach the security threshold. The agent surveys my license, looking twice as if the resemblance is of question. I can't smile, my face frozen. Finally, deciding I look enough like the photo to at least allow me to step forward, he stamps the boarding pass and hands it back with disinterest, already addressing the couple behind me.

Relieved to cross the first threshold, I step forward, stripping shoes, jacket, lifting the bag of acceptable bottles out and laying it in the bin. Motioned to the gate, I step through and the attendant smiles, then the beeper goes off.

I have been selected for random special scrutiny. I am directed into the Plexiglas box where I am to wait for an agent. The clear plastic box leaves me under observation by all proceeding passengers who are waved on by.

First, I pace from one end to the other, doing my best imitation of Darth Maul waiting for battle, staring at fellow travelers who pass unimpeded. Then I start yelling. Then I sit down and begin shedding clothes. An attendant steps to the front of the gate and asks me to calm down. I scream obscenities and demand to be let out of the box.

Before I have stripped to embarrassing dimensions, a sweaty man stuffed into a TSA uniform opens the Plexiglas prison's door and waves me out. He motions to my bags and orders me to open them, then paws through my belongings, hunting for secret compartments.

Finding nothing except my ratty underwear and extra jeans, he orders me to show him my hands. He wipes them or runs something over them, I'm so angry I'm not tracking now, and know only that he has touched me in some way and I want to kill him. I'm no longer breathing; I'm inhaling and exhaling the universe in fury.

The alarm goes off. A woman in a uniform steps forward telling me I have explosive residue on my hands. I now need a complete pat down. I'm losing it.

"EXPLOSIVES! ARE YOU ALL OUT OF YOUR MINDS?" I raise the roof.

The lady agent tells me it might be household cleanser residue; sometimes the machine sets off for these too.

"AND WHICH SEEMS MORE LIKELY?!!!!" I continue making a spectacle of myself.

"Please come with us, we need to finish the inspection."

She motions towards a little room in which she will pat me down.

Oh no, you won't. Touch me and I will kill you.

"OH FINE, SO NOW YOU TAKE ME IN THE BACK AND FEEL ME UP. GREAT, YOU SICK PERVERTS."

That's it for lady agent. She motions to the police. I can't help but pray that this time I'll be brave enough to make them shoot me, rather than let them take me in. But I start to cry, and I blurt out that I have been gang-raped, and I can't stand the idea of strangers touching me.

I'm actually making this up. I have no idea why I'm having this tantrum. I've been through security many times, and this is not the first time I have had to stand spread-eagle while creeps-in-uniform feel me up. I have been nauseous and impatient before, but this is the first time I've lost it.

Lady agent waves off the officers and tells me in a matter-of-fact tone that she also has been raped, and you just have to get over it, as she has. I don't point out to her that now she is the one molesting strangers under color-of-law, not the one being molested with apparent color-of-law protection, so her perspective is off, but I stand with arms outstretched and let her get it over with. The cops stand down.

I am sent on my way worse for the wear. I swear that if I can't kill someone soon, someone who really deserves it, I cannot inhabit this meat sack much longer, too much anger, too much fear, too much hate.

Big Sis is out of town, but I stay at her house this time, not at my mother's. I've stayed here many times. Big Sis shares the house with her partner, a Vietnam veteran. We've known each other nearly twenty years.

I arrive still consumed with rage. I curse and spit and rail at the indignity and my own horrible behavior. I pace the house in fury vowing to never be seen again in public, to never allow anyone to touch me or to see me or to…ever.

I rage on. He listens and watches, occasionally offering food and other treats. I rage and cry.

Finally, a few hours in, when I have collapsed in exhaustion and curled into a ball in the soft armchair, he offers this, "Things don't ever seem to work out for you, do they? Maybe you've got P.T.S.D."

I've wondered about this but no one else has ever suggested it. I know my war veteran friends are being diagnosed with it. I know they too have trouble keeping jobs, staying married, facing the world, that homelessness and suicide rates among them are making society's failures painfully obvious.

His observation that nothing works out for me rings too painfully true. He confirms that I'm a failure, that I just can't seem to cut it. But he also plants a seed of hope that maybe there is an explanation, one I might understand before I give up for good. The idea saves me momentarily. In my moment of grace, I was tasked with understanding, not repair.

I appreciate the time with my mother. She is cordial although she spends time chatting with invisible visitors so I am not certain she knows I'm actually present. We both survive my short stint.

I return home without incident, although at the airport I have to stop and ask for a glass of water—standing and moving is very difficult—and I arrive home to my apartment in dread of the next day. I have to die or go to work, and I just can't work; I don't want anyone to see me. I can't pretend I want to do anything but die.

The pets save me. Although I had decided before the trip that I would kill them and then myself, I can't kill them. I love them, and if it isn't love that they return, it's an acceptable imitation, and for their ability to share it, I can't hurt them.

I look for help once again in therapy, looking for someone who will help me find the courage to return to work or enough trust to leave the pets in someone else's care. This second option now seems reasonable.

I'm limited to inexpensive therapy, having few resources. My community offers a service related to therapists-in-training. Within this group, I ask for someone familiar with Post-Traumatic Stress Disorder. I decide I might as well find out what it is, and if perhaps it might explain why I live a life so marred and so similar to my Vietnam veteran acquaintances.

Once we have a match, I schedule an appointment with a woman nearing the end of her internship who is experienced with P.T.S.D. I ask to be seen for depression.

The day arrives. I need the counseling, but wish I didn't. I hate running through the whole story. No one seems to listen beyond the first sentence, or so it seems given listeners seem to make assumptions that have no relation to what I've just said or proceed to ask questions that have been expressly answered. I assume in the first few minutes they are too busy assessing their own danger to truly listen.

I prepare. First, I stare into the closet. I can't decide what to wear; nothing seems right. I remember a day long ago when Little Sis had a seizure. I was home alone with her, and as she went limp, I stood staring at the closet like this, struggling with what a nine-year-old should wear for a run next door to plead for help. The dilemma is different this time, but the stress the same.

I know the therapist will draw conclusions from my appearance. I've watched them assess me many times: too casual—bag lady, failing self care; too much skin—slut, hyper sexualized; too buttoned down—well, too buttoned down.

I settle on jeans and a T-shirt—17-year-old, emotionally immature. We can start there.

The office building is modest. I struggle to get the front door open, autumn winds so strong they keep it pressed firmly shut. A gentleman opens it from the inside and invites me to sit in the small waiting room.

I rehearse my story as I wait, trying to keep it concise and helpful. A dark-haired young woman in a black suit sees a patient out of her nearby office, then introduces herself and we begin.

We exchange pleasantries, and I complete paperwork, answering the by-now familiar questionnaire measuring my current state of despondency. I finish and hand it back.

She sits at her desk, flipping through the pile, noting my checkmarks, confirming my diagnosis: depression. Turning her attention away from the paperwork, she sets the pile aside and turns to me.

My diagnosis and emotional state raise troubling issues for a therapist. Should I hurt myself or someone else, that poor soul bears some potential legal responsibility, enough that the call for hospitalization rests with them, if they're sure.

That puts me in danger as far as I'm concerned. I only enter this relationship in desperation. I have no intention of relinquishing rights, and I haven't changed my opinion on the matter. No one will ever again hold me anywhere without my consent, and no one is getting it. I am a terrible patient.

I know what comes next, she has to handle me, and if I am to get any honest help at all, I have to handle back.

Her face somber, she leans forward in her chair, lowering both her head and her voice, "Do you have any current plans to harm yourself?"

The truth is out of the question. I look away. We'll do the dance.

"I know you have to report it, if I'm a danger to myself or anyone else. So I will answer no. They put you in an impossible position, don't they?"

She defers the obvious and asks instead, "What would you do if I feel I have to report it?"

I look at her for a moment. I hate her because I need help, and she seems much too kind. The hostility is unintended, but I'm not at my best.

"I'll use the pen in my purse to slit my throat before you make a call or leave the room."

I win. Ground rules are set. She has me sign a contract that I won't do anything drastic.

Sure.

She isn't interested in back story. Beyond "gang rape," she never asks, and I never tell. We deal with now. First, she works on bonding and calming me down. We sit on the floor and meditate, much like lying on the floor in English class at Orange Coast listening to rock and roll. I'm fully cooperative. I can do this.

She sends me home with Pema Chodron CDs, and encourages me to Be Here Now, renamed Mindfulness in this day and age. The appointments remind me of earlier days when therapy for post-partum depression became existential. Though I've never made it beyond page three, I still own *The Course in Miracles.*

Eventually, as fall turns to winter, I stop crying and calm down enough to listen.

She has never asked to hear the story of my kidnapping, but she tells me she is a survivor of sexual assault herself, and she believes I have P.T.S.D. She sends me home from this appointment with materials to read and workbooks to complete.

I go home and read, embarrassed and amazed to discover how closely the profile fits me. Post-Traumatic Stress Disorder: brain damage as the result of trauma exacerbated by societal failings, resulting in chronic difficulty and fractured lives. *Why don't I know this? Where was I?* I am a walking cliché. *How did this get by me?*

As with the twenty-year-late notice that I am no longer deemed a liar, the information doesn't undo the harm, but it does give me my first glimmer of hope in what has been a 40-year saga, that if I am not all right, perhaps it is not entirely my fault.

The emotional benefit from this knowledge will perhaps come later, but the immediate implication of the diagnosis: I might be entitled to Social Security disability. In the short term at least, I could be spared another job hunt without fear of ending up homeless.

The very idea is so wonderful that I'm afraid to hope. I complete pages of forms and questionnaires. Apparently the inability to hold a job is one symptom. I need an extra page to list my former employers, my credibility unquestionable. Ultimately, I'm directed to medical appointments.

I meet separately with three practitioners, their specific credentials unclear, each name followed by sufficient abbreviations to reassure and impress, or in my case to confuse, but the process is familiar. I complete the now-familiar questionnaires—how dangerous are you?—and then we chat.

I try my best to be honest. No one here has more interest in the truth than I, but I do keep in mind that they can lock me up, if I give them any reason to fear me. "Too nice to kill" is on display, a balance of forthright and cautious.

Despite what I consider to be polite restraint on my part, by the end of the appointment each doctor seems amazed that I am out and about. After examination, they all express surprise that I am not dead or in prison, or at least in need of addiction rehab. Apparently, I should be even crazier than I am.

They all suggest hospitalization, offering to admit me immediately. I have succeeded in convincing them I am rational enough to make the decision myself, but when I decline, they make certain I have transportation home, again a little surprised that I am driving myself around. They are solicitous and a little frightening.

The verdict is yes, I have Post-Traumatic Stress Disorder, and I have earned Social Security disability. In the immediate future, I will not starve, and I don't have to face another job hunt. The doctors tell me to relax; the offer for hospitalization remains open.

The envelope with the decision arrives in the late afternoon. I carry it to the meadow and sit on a log beside the creek. Daisy wades. It's still chilly, but spring is softening the world, green sprigs and tiny white flowers poke through the brown grasses blanketing the field behind me.

I reread the disability award letter with the diagnosis. It is not my imagination. I do not experience the world in the same way as do non-injured people, but more importantly for my Self, I am not a failure for having been unable to "get over it." I was never going to be able to talk myself out of it.

Best, I won't have to explain myself again. I'll need no more conversations that imply I am just sad because my dreams didn't come true, or that I'm ashamed because I enjoyed the rape sex, or that my anger is mere indignation because I valued myself so highly.

The diagnosis doesn't cure me. I still avoid participation in the wider world. I don't sleep well, and I get sick to my stomach facing unfamiliar territory, but I don't feel so guilty about it anymore.

The vindication frees me. Knowing what causes the rattle doesn't eliminate it, but the nerves themselves no longer frighten me. Of course I'm afraid in public; the world is an unpredictable place. That I find it unnerving is neither character flaw nor personality disorder. I can stop feeling ashamed.

I embrace my loved ones and attempt to explain the diagnosis to them. They embrace me back and try to understand it. For the first time in decades I travel with my daughter and we attend my son's wedding far away with many strangers. I can't eat more than a few bites at any meal, but it doesn't matter so much. I love my new family members anyway.

My daughter and I laugh together through travel mishaps and language barriers and in a wondrous setting celebrate a joyful marriage, one full of youth's plans and dreams.

I stand with her in the Alps as the summer evening closes around us, toasting the new couple, and I cry without guilt. A gift of such beauty is beyond any hope I ever held. I am so glad I stayed around to see what would happen next. It turns out, I am fine, really.

Post Script

A few details remained to be addressed in this manuscript, this overgrown suicide note, when I decided to visit Little Sis for a few days. One such detail involved the badges on the front of a motorcycle-club jacket: are they "colors?" I have considered calling a Harley Davidson dealership and asking a salesman or pulling up next to a Hells Angel on a roadway to ask, but haven't yet, when I set out to visit my sister.

On the drive to her new home, out of state, I pull off at a highway rest-stop between here and there, missing Daisy in the seat beside me as the car comes to a stop. She stayed home. I'm hundreds of miles from anywhere I've ever been.

As I step out of the car to stretch my legs, motorcycles roar in from the highway, filling the remaining parking spaces around me. The riders of the huge bikes wearing their leather jackets, their colors, the Soul Brothers motorcycle club has just pulled in.

This is the same club whose president blocked my path outside my sister's garage and offered to avenge my kidnapping forty years ago, a gesture of kindness I still treasure. I haven't seen any of them in all these years. It is the badges on their jackets that have me searching for words.

As the men heft themselves off their bikes, I dance around among them, trying to introduce myself, exclaiming in amazement at their arrival, babbling out the reason as best I can. As I sputter and twirl, an older rider steps up from the group and removes his helmet. He's one of the men who offered to help. He was there. He remembers me.

We cry and hug, both astounded and delighted by the coincidence. They have been at a rally out of state and are on their way home to the Bay Area. He shares news of the others, the elders, some are well, some are not. A Vietnam veteran himself, he tells me he's just been diagnosed with P.T.S.D.

I ask my question about the jackets, and they all pitch in to answer. No, the badges are not colors.

We part ways at the rest stop, leaving me with a certainty that something is going on here. Still left with absolutely no idea what it is, but something, truly.

I'm sure of it.

Acknowledgements

Thank you to those who have helped me complete this book. In particular: Instructor *Janet Lee Carey* for her high compliment; Editors *Adele Becker, Gloria Campbell,* and *Rachael Logan* for their guidance, encouragement, and kindness along the way; and to my early readers, whose responses kept me going, *T, Lisa, Adrienne* and *Ghislaine*. I would not, nor could not, have done it without you.

CPSIA information can be obtained
at www.ICGtesting.com
Printed in the USA
LVOW12s0107090517
533706LV00002B/553/P

9 780998 669502